Craving Cookies

The Quintessential American Cookie Book

by Helen S. Fletcher

Dedication

For my cookie loving husband Mike. When you have spent
sixty years married to the same person, it is special –
as are you. I am grateful!

Previous Books by Helen S. Fletcher
The New Pastry Cook,
European Tarts,

Blog, Pastries Like a Pro at www.pastrieslikeapro.com

For information about this title or to order other books and/or electronic media, contact the publisher:

Helen S. Fletcher
St. Louis, Missouri
email: pastrieslikeapro@gmail.com
website: www.pastrieslikeapro.com

ISBN
978-1-7354284-0-6 (paperback)
978-1-7354284-1-3 (ebook)

Printed in the United States of America

Cover photos: Sienna Lace, Peppermint Ravioli, Inside out Oreos, Crème de Menthe Patties

Photos by: T. Mike Fletcher, Helen S. Fletcher

Cover and Interior design: Dan & Darlene Swanson of Van-garde Imagery, Inc. • van-garde.com

Table of Contents

Foreword

I AM THRILLED TO WRITE the foreword for Helen Fletcher's new cookbook, *Craving Cookies: The Quintessential American Cookie Book*. I first got to know Helen through her blog *Pastries Like a Pro*, a site that is a reflex of her deep knowledge about baking and her commitment to teaching it to others. Baking can be intimidating because so many details matter, and so many recipes are misleading. Often authors simplify things too much to make them less daunting, but important details are left out. Or they go the opposite route, complicating every single step so much that the whole process seems too difficult to bother with. Helen strikes the perfect balance. She shares all details that you need to pay attention to when baking her recipes, and if you do that, you will be successful every single time, no matter how complex the bake might be.

Her new cookbook starts with a solid chapter on the techniques that will be employed throughout the book, and then dives into sections according to the type of bake: many types of cookies (Cut Out, Drop Cookies, Meringue, to name a few), followed by a large collection of brownies and bars. You will find not only the American classics we know and love, but versions in which she opens our horizons with exciting new flavors and ideas.

Helen is a natural teacher, and her passion for baking transpires in her writing. If I could, I would love to be a student in her professional kitchen. Unfortunately, that is not possible, but reading her cookbooks is a close second to that dream. Every recipe teaches me something, every little tip she shares makes my baking better. No matter the level of expertise, anyone will benefit from her great recipes and vast baking knowledge.

Sally Newton

Acknowledgements for *Craving Cookies*

DESPITE THE MANY HOURS SPENT shopping, testing, retesting, writing, and reading content over and over in search of a missing comma, forgotten measurement, or that one photo that needs a bit of help, no one writes a book by themselves.

Many people have contributed to the final book that is now in your hands or on your screen. To that end, I owe many people my thanks for helping me get this published.

First, my husband Mike. Luckily for me he is retired, and as such, he helped immensely with the shopping, photography, and the ever-present clean-up. He was also my main taste-tester, and I'm happy to say he enjoyed every single one of the cookies! But in saying that, I must divulge that he was the only one who enjoyed my pumpkin soup one Thanksgiving where everyone else politely pushed it around their bowls after only one bite. That qualifies as true love!

Several people helped with reading the recipes for spelling and punctuation, including, Janet Laudenschlager and John Wilson. If I didn't adequately convey my appreciation then, please accept my enduring thanks now.

Craving Cookies in its final form would not have been possible without the keen eye and dedication of Sara Garfinkel, who asked a myriad of questions to ensure that every sentence and recipe was made easy to understand. I love working with young people and Sara and I share a special connection. Her dedication to working on this book was admirable, especially on the tight time frame we had. Her constant cheerful support was very welcomed as I sometimes felt swamped from biting off more than I could chew all at once. Thank you, Sara.

The last person to check the book was Kate Fletcher. Her keen eye found what others of us missed. In doing so, their help was invaluable. Thank you Kate.

To my book designer, Darlene Swanson, who took a bunch of words and pictures and turned them into a book that reflects my approach to how a cookbook should present itself to readers and users - I appreciate your talent. I was lucky to find Darlene and be able to work with her. I'm amazed by her ability to transform the words and photographs into a book that I hope will be used for years and years by my readers. In addition, Dan Swanson designed the gorgeous cover – thank you Dan. You know I love it.

To everyone along the way who encouraged me, helped me, and just were there for me when I needed you, thank you. You are as much a part of this book as I am.

Helen S. Fletcher

Craving Cookies Introduction

As a professional baker and pastry chef for over thirty years, it has always amazed me that cookies have been relegated to the bottom rung when it comes to the baking and pastry arts.

With the exception of Christmas, when cookies are king, they seem to be taken for granted. And it's not that everyone doesn't love them; on the contrary, they are loved. Much loved!

For me, cookies have always remained high on my list since I started baking. I treasure the handwritten recipes for European cookies left by my mother, back when baking took far more time than it does today with our high-speed mixers and processors. I can still see her cranking her tiny little mouli grater with all of its inter-changeable drums, a world away from whizzing nuts in a processor or quickly making a dough like *Shortbread* as we do today.

When I first mentioned that I was writing a book devoted to cookies, one of my blog readers asked why I thought the world needed another cookie book. It was a fair question that caused me to think about cookies as a whole. First, I think cookies are more popular than ever, as they fall into one of two categories. There are those cookies that are gorgeous works of art, with intricacies and decoration reflecting the talent of a true artist, but aren't really meant to be eaten.

That's not me and is not what this book is about. Craving Cookies falls into the second category of cookie, the one where they are meant to be eaten with gusto and shared - or not! Therein lies the secret to their popularity. Cookies are casual, fitting easily into today's lifestyle. Of all things baking and pastry, cookies are manageable for anyone - easy, versatile, and adaptable.

Cookies can provide comfort, flavor, familiarity, or a sense of the exotic all in a bite or two. They can be sub-lime and subtle, or ridiculous and over-the-top, or elegant and simple. They can have a place at the greatest of celebrations or simply keep us company when we are home alone on a gray day.

I didn't grow up wildly excited about spending time in the kitchen baking with my mother, although she and my grandmother were marvelous bakers. I was much happier living my childhood as best friends with my brother and being the biggest tomboy ever. Mud pies were the closest I got to anything resembling making food!

It wasn't until after I married that I went to my mother and grandmother, both from Europe, to teach me how to cook and bake. Their skills were amazing, and the cookies were unlike anything American. I learned quickly and it became evident that baking was my favorite.

Christmas was cookie time, as it was in so many homes, and I kept that tradition going. I would bake hundreds of cookies in all shapes, sizes, textures, and flavors. My greatest joy was being in the kitchen at night, after my boys were in bed and the house was quiet. There was something magical about taking flour, butter, sugar, eggs, nuts, and flavorings and turning them into a multitude of treasured bites that would come around once a year. There were rolled cookies, shaped cookies, cut-out cookies, drop cookies, and bars as beautiful as those for sale in any bakery. I loved seeing them cover the large dining room table, just waiting to be boxed, wrapped, and shipped to loved ones across the country, blissfully knowing the joy those boxes would bring when opened.

After my boys were just about out of high school, I decided to use my love of baking to open an upscale wholesale bakery servicing hotels, restaurants, and caterers. Having no professional baking or business experience at the time, the learning curve was very steep and, truth to tell, I almost fell off a couple of times. I was intent on hand baking in small batches with only the best ingredients, using no preservatives and offering the best possible version of whatever I was making. At the time, bakeries didn't bake this way, and I was told over and over that I wouldn't succeed... But succeed I did! After three years, the shop had to expand to keep up with the business; and then again eighteen months after that. We added wedding cakes, and along with these cakes we made thousands and thousands of cookies as favors for the guests.

When I opened the retail take out shop, of course cakes and pastries were offered. But among the most popular offerings were our *Painted Cookies*. Brightly colored Christmas designs sat beside Jewish menorahs and dreidels in December. Spring featured baskets of flowers, Easter bunnies, and painted eggs. Summer produced glowing suns, Fourth of July flags, and beach buckets. The fall season saw leaves, acorns, and of course, lots of Halloween designs. These colorful cookies along with the myriad shortbreads, filled cookies, brownies, and bars never failed to please our customers, who would often buy them as gifts. It was a source of great pleasure to see their happiness in buying the cookies, watching them wonder which ones to pick and, more often than not, succumb to buying more than they set out to purchase.

Modern methods of making cookies serve as the perfect introduction to baking. Simple cookies such as *Shortbreads* with only three ingredients, or the *Peanut Butter Bars* requiring no baking, can spark an interest in cookies that will last a lifetime, just as they have done for me.

 Many American cookies and bars have a lot of add-ins that make for a more complex cookie and a more daunting ingredient list. You've heard of the phrase, the more the merrier? That often applies here. Granulated sugar and/or brown sugar are the most often used sweeteners. Salt and leavening agents such as baking powder and baking soda are most prevalent in American cookies. Whole eggs are used more often than just egg yolks. As for nuts, anything goes - From the ones indigenous to the Americas such as peanuts and pecans, to hazelnuts, macadamias, almonds, pistachios, walnuts, and a variety of seeds. Chocolate is a huge addition in American cookies as a filling, glaze, or as the cookie itself. Vanilla is the predominant flavoring favored by Americans.

I'm never happy with just following a recipe; I always try to find a way to make them easier, more consistent, or just to add variation. I get excited about teaching and sharing what I find. I approach every recipe as though I am standing next to someone who is a novice to baking. Starting with cookies is ideal. They are generally the easiest of all baking and pastry endeavors, which perhaps is why they are taken for granted. Where I can, I have sought to simplify the techniques by updating the mixing and shaping of the cookies and using modern equipment.

Sharing this collection of cookies, as well as introducing new and exciting ones such as the *Orange Pistachio Delights* and *Peppermint Raviolis*, has made me realize just how much I love making and sharing my recipes. The fun of creating a new cookie remains just one of the reasons I will always love to bake and share.

This book is my personal journey through the world of cookies. It is not inclusive of every American cookie, but those that most appeal to me, as well as ones I have created along the way. I like bold flavors in my cookies; an unexpected hint of black pepper in a spice mix or a bit of cayenne with chocolate ups the flavor and intensifies the pleasure. My love affair with cookies is all-inclusive and nondiscriminatory, I love both a simple butter cookie and one jam-packed with fruits, nuts, and chocolate – always chocolate!

While cookies are among the easiest of all baking projects, there are still details that can and will make all the difference in the outcome. It gives me great pleasure to share what I have learned in my many years of baking at home and professionally. ◆

A Word About the Photography

I HAVE A FIRMLY HELD belief about learning, and that is that seeing how something works, like watching a technique or viewing photos, is just as important as the words themselves.

To that end, each recipe in this book has a photo of the finished cookie. Some recipes, where words alone would not adequately convey the directions, have a set of photos as a guide.

In order to ensure your success with these recipes, and to make this the most accurate guide possible, all of the photos in this book were provided by my husband or myself. The photography was done on-site, at the time the recipes were made. This was done in an effort to convey the truest sense of how a cookie should look when finished, as well as include a sequence of how-to photos where needed. These are just my cookies, photographed in my kitchen.

I am lucky to be married to a man who was a freelance professional photographer prior to retirement. He traveled the world, viewing it through the lens of his camera and recording the sights for his many clients. Mike's work in editorials, ads, and annual reports did not include food photography, but his contributions to my career in food are many.

I would also like to thank my son Dirk, also a professional in the world of photography, for all of his assistance and encouragement as he helped me learn the ins-and-outs of making a visual account of the recipes. ♦

Cookie Baking Equipment

MAKING COOKIES REQUIRES SOME EQUIPMENT, but not a lot. Some of the cookies in this book can be made using only a bowl, a few measuring utensils, a whisk, and a pan. I am listing the equipment I use in this book for reference.

When I first started baking, I didn't necessarily have every piece listed, but bought them as I needed them.

Measuring Equipment

Of every piece of equipment listed in this section, the scale is the most important. It is the only way to achieve consistent results every time. Cup sizes may vary, but a gram is a gram and an ounce is an ounce. I use grams simply because they are easier to use than ounces, which will often have partial numbers. Grams will always be in whole numbers.

There is a difference between wet and dry measuring cups. Wet measuring cups have a pouring spout, and the last marked measure usually doesn't come to the very top of the cup. Dry measures are made so they can be overfilled and the excess swept off with the back of a knife for a precise measure.

Left to Right - Back row: Wet measures, scale. Front row: Dry measures, measuring spoons.

Disher/Scoopers

These marvelous tools are perfect for portioning cookie dough in different sizes. I used four sizes of disher/scoopers in this book, but also give an equivalent measure in case you don't have these. They are sized in ascending order with the smallest number being the largest scooper.

Left to Right: Numbers 40, 60, 70, and 100

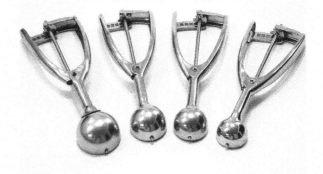

#40 disher/scooper = 1½ tablespoons
#60 disher/scooper = 1 tablespoon
#70 disher/scooper = 2¾ teaspoons
#100 disher/scooper = 2 teaspoons

Baking Sheets

Ever since owning the bakery, the only baking sheets I use are sheet pans. Sheet pans have a ¾ to 1 inch edge around the sides making them ideal for bars and cookies. These are the sizes I use in this book:

Half sheet pan (18x13 inch)
Quarter sheet pan (13x9 inch)
Jelly Roll pan (10x15¼ inch)

Most pans used in baking are aluminum because it conducts heat evenly and will last a lifetime if kept well. Look for 12 to 18 gauge aluminum to prevent warping when heated or frozen, which can occur if it is a lighter gauge. It is often difficult to find the gauge of a sheet pan because the number is not on the pan itself. Ordering through the internet can make it easier to know what you are getting; simply search for a heavy gauge or a specified number.

Deep Baking Pans

Bars and brownies can require deeper pans than sheet pans. The sizes used in this book are 8x8x2, 9x9x2, 9x13x2, and 10x13 inch pans.

Mixing Equipment

Many of these cookies can be mixed with a strong arm and a spoon, but most of us these days opt for a mixer. There are hand mixers that will work fine if the dough is not too stiff or if the batch is not too big, but my mixer of choice is a stand mixer. They are much more powerful and can handle heavier loads.

I, quite frankly, could not live without this second mixing machine… A food processor. As a previous consultant to Cuisinart, I saw just how many chores this machine is capable of doing, and I have religiously used one ever since, even to the point of adapting many of my recipes to using it via my blog, www.pastrieslikeapro.com.

Last, but not least, is a simple whisk. A whisk can be used to mix portions of recipes or even a recipe in its entirety, so make sure to buy a sturdy one.

Left to Right: Food processor, stand mixer. Whisk in front.

Back row: Marble rolling pin on its cradle. Middle row: Various cookie cutters. Front row: Pastry wheel.

A marble rolling pin is particularly good because it is cooler than a wooden one, but either is fine. See see page xxxi for information on the cut-out cookie technique.

Spatulas

There are several different kinds of spatulas. The metal ones, which should have a bit of flex to them, include a large and small straight spatula (the small straight spatula is not shown), as well as a large and small offset spatula used for spreading batter and frostings. The red bowl scraper makes it super easy to get cookie dough out of the mixer in one fell swoop, leaving the bowl completely clean. The white rubber spatula is not rigid, it has some flex in it, and the hard plastic spatula is particularly useful for the processor. Don't use a rubber or soft plastic spatula in the processor because it can cut up quickly when scraping the bowl. One last useful spatula is a high-heat spatula for stirring things on the stove. As you can see in the photo, mine is green, making it super easy to find when I need it.

Pastry Tips/Brushes

It is often easier to use a pastry bag and tips to pipe filling or shape cookies than it is to do without. I prefer disposable plastic pastry bags. The bag's corner needs to be cut off to accommodate the tip. It is important to note that simply cutting the end off of a pastry bag and using without a tip can be problematic because the end will stretch. The metal tip prevents this from occurring.

Brushes have a variety of uses in a baker's kitchen, including washing down crystals when making caramel and wetting the edges of dough.

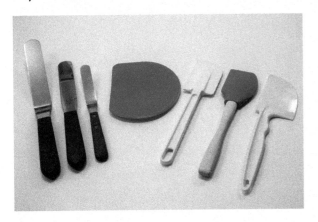

Left to Right: Large offset metal spatula, straight metal spatula, small offset spatula, red bowl scraper, white rubber spatula, green high-heat spatula, hard plastic spatula for the processor.

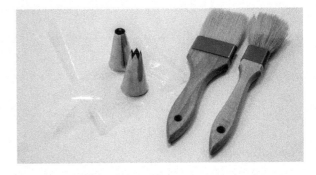

Cut-Out Cookies

A rolling pin and cookie cutters are used for cut-out cookies, as well as a pastry wheel or pizza cutter if squares or rectangles are being cut with fluted edges.

Left to Right: A disposable plastic pastry bag under two pastry tips - The one in the back is a plain tip, the one in the front is an open star tip. Pastry brushes.

Paper Goods

Parchment paper makes baking so much easier. No more greasing or spraying pans, simply lay down a piece of paper and place your cookies on top. Worried about getting those bars out of the pan? Line the pan with parchment paper and you're all set.

Wax paper is particularly helpful for rolling dough and cutting cookies. See see page xlii for more on this technique.

Plastic wrap and foil have their place in baking, too.

Another item that can make your life so much easier is cake boards. They can be found in both rounds and rectangles online. Cake boards make it so easy to release bars and brownies from their pans without damaging them. There are both waxed and unwaxed boards; if you purchase the waxed ones, they can often be wiped down and used again.

Back to Front: Plastic wrap, film, wax paper, parchment paper. Cake board is under the parchment paper.

Miscellaneous

This is sort of a catchall for various odds and ends that are useful.

Cake testers and timers are self-explanatory.

Left to Right - Top row: Blow dryer, timer. Bottom row: Strainer, cake tester, instant read thermometer, serrated knife, microplane grater.

An oven thermometer used from time to time will ensure that the oven is at the correct temperature. If it is not, lower or raise the temperature as necessary. An instant read thermometer that goes up to 350°F / 175°C is also good for checking temperature when making caramel and sugar syrups, as these require specificity.

A microplane grater is wonderful for zesting or grating citrus fruits. It is so much easier and better than using a box grater.

I use a strainer to sift ingredients together, or, in the case of cake flour and cocoa, to always sift when called for. These ingredients have a tendency to clump, and if they are not sifted, can remain as undissolved lumps in the finished batter or dough.

A serrated knife, with its sawtoothed edge, is often better at making clean cuts than using a straight-edged knife, specifically when cutting through the top of bar cookies. Pair this knife with a sawing motion for professional-looking cuts.

So, you ask, what is a blow dryer doing in a cookie book? Well, it's used to release bars and brownies when they cling to the pan, of course! See see page xxxix for more on this technique. ◆

Ingredients

THIS COMPENDIUM RELATES TO THE ingredients used in this book. While I have mentioned some of the ingredients by specific brand name, there are others that also work well. Not everything is available in every area.

Almond flour is made from ground almonds. While it can be made at home by processing nuts with a bit of the sugar or flour from the recipe, it will never be as finely ground as a commercial product. Macaroons and gluten-free cookies are much better when made with purchased almond flour. Be sure to look for the words "finely ground." Almond flour can clump. Simply run it through a food processor to return it to a fine powder. Sift before using. Because nuts are high in oil, flour made from them can easily become rancid. Store the flour in the freezer.

Almond paste is made with ground almonds, sugar and glycerin (or other liquids), and is sometimes flavored with almond extract. It should not be confused with marzipan, which is similar, but sweeter and bound with egg whites. Marzipan is used in decorations; it can be rolled out and applied to cakes, just as fondant is used. Almond paste is an ingredient while marzipan is a final product.

Ammonium carbonate or baker's ammonia is the leavening agent of choice in European cookies and crackers. Always make sure you are using food grade ammonium.

Ammonium carbonate is used when the end product is crispy, such as crackers and crunchy cookies. It produces an airy texture that neither baking powder nor baking soda can achieve. This texture is created when the tiny crystals dissolve during baking, leaving very small air cells, making it easier for the moisture to escape. In addition, only a clean taste remains, none of the soapy aftertaste that baking powder or baking soda can sometmes leave. In a recipe, less ammonium carbonate is used than baking soda or baking powder.

Ammonium carbonate has the same strong pungent odor that is found in smelling salts. Don't sniff when opening the bottle. It won't harm you, but it is extremely sharp and off-putting. Interestingly enough, the odor completely dissipates when baked, although it can be detected to some degree as the cookies bake. For some cookies, this is the only leavening agent to use. It can be found online.

Store ammonium carbonate in a cool, dark place. It is susceptible to caking and drying. If this happens, use a table knife or ice pick to break it up, then crush it under a knife or a meat tenderizer to turn it back into powder. Ammonium carbonate is dissolved in liquid before adding to other ingredients. It will fizz quite a bit when added to the liquid and then will subside.

Ascorbic acid can be found as a stand-alone product and is also contained in Vitamin C tablets. The powder is used to add tang to replicate the flavor of citrus. If using Vitamin C, crush the tablets into a powder and sift to remove any large pieces.

Baking powder is a leavening agent consisting of baking soda, an acid such as cream of tartar, and a moisture-absorbing ingredient such as cornstarch. When mixed with a liquid, carbon dioxide gas is released, causing the product to rise. There are two types of baking powder: **Single acting baking powder** releases its gas as soon as moisture is introduced. **Double acting baking powder** releases part of its gas when moisture is introduced, and the remainder when heat is applied. Double acting baking powder is the most commonly used and can be easily found on supermarket shelves. It should be kept in a cool, dry place because it is perishable. To determine whether baking powder is fresh, add 1 teaspoon to ⅓ cup hot water. It should bubble vigorously. If it doesn't bubble, discard and replace. I recommend using aluminum-free baking powder, such as Rumford or Argo. There are other brands available as well.

In a pinch, **baking powder can be made** by combining one part baking soda to one part cornstarch and two parts cream of tartar. To make 1 teaspoon, use ¼ teaspoon baking soda, ¼ teaspoon cornstarch and ½ teaspoon cream of tartar. Sift together several times to make sure they are well combined. Use immediately. The ratio is twice as much cream of tartar as baking soda.

Baking soda, known chemically as sodium bicarbonate, requires an acid to activate. When moisture is added, it forms bubbles of carbon dioxide. If baking soda is used alone, that acid has to come from other ingredients in the recipe, such as buttermilk, lemon juice, vinegar, honey, molasses, brown sugar, natural cocoa, yogurt, or sour cream. When heated, the baking soda forms sodium carbonate, which can have an unpleasant aftertaste. The acid in the recipe helps to neutralize this. When the acid and baking soda are combined and heated in the oven, carbon

dioxide is released, thus resulting in a lightened, or leavened, product. Baking soda should be sifted before use because it has a tendency to clump. The clumps don't always dissolve in the mixture.

Brandy is a liquor distilled from wine or fermented fruit juice. It is aged in wood, which contributes to its flavor and color.

Butter is made by churning cream until it separates into a semisolid and a liquid. If you care to experiment, butter can be made at home by whipping heavy cream in a mixer or food processor until it turns to butter. On August 31, 1989 the United States Department of Agriculture (USDA) established standards for grades of American butter based on flavor, body, texture, color, and salt (if present). It must be at least 80% milk fat with the remaining 20% water and milk solids. The grades are based on a score of 100 with AA being the finest at 93, A at 92, and B at 90. AA and A are the most commonly available.

European or European-style butter is a cultured butter, and has a higher milk fat content, about 82%. Because of the culture, it has an intensely-rich and tangy butter flavor. While it used to be imported — hence the name — high-fat butter is now made domestically, mainly by smaller craft dairies. This butter is ideal for use in butter cookies, or whenever there aren't a lot of competing ingredients.

Butter may be colored with annatto, a type of food coloring made from the achiote tree, and can be salted or unsalted. This is often referred to as sweet butter. Salt is used as a preservative, so salted butter will stay fresher longer than unsalted butter. If buying unsalted butter in a quantity you cannot use within two weeks, you can preserve its flavor and freshness by freezing it. Butter absorbs flavors around it, so it should be stored tightly wrapped. The recipes in this book use unsalted butter.

When a recipe calls for softened butter, the temperature should be between 70°F-72°F / 22°C-23°C. If it is colder, the butter won't cream properly. It will resemble wet sand. If it is warmer, the butter gets too soft and runs the risk of melting, which will change the texture of the finished cookie. I don't use the term "room temperature" for butter because some rooms are cold and some are very warm. Neither one is great for softened butter. The butter should yield under your finger; your finger shouldn't go through! The temperature of melted butter is approximately 85°F-90°F / 29°C-32°C.

If you're in a hurry, do not microwave butter unless it is at half power, and even then only in very short bursts. A better shortcut is to cut the butter into quarter-inch slices or smaller, and place them in a single layer on a plate while you prepare everything else for the recipe. The butter should be soft and ready when you need it.

Brown butter is used as a flavoring agent. It is made by heating butter until it comes to a boil. Reduce the heat to a simmer, and cook until the milk solidifies. It will drop to the bottom of the pan and turn a golden brown. Care must be taken because the solids can go from golden to burned very quickly.

Candied orange peel is the peel of an orange cooked in a sugar syrup. It can be rolled in granulated sugar or left plain. Trader Joe's has candied orange slices that actually taste like oranges. These are preferred over the little containers that appear around Christmas and used in fruitcake. An extremely easy method of making candied orange peel

can be found on my blog at http://www.pastries-likeapro.com/.

Chocolate comes from the tropical cacao tree. The beans are separated from their pods, fermented, dried, roasted, then cracked to remove the nibs. They are ground to remove about 75% cocoa butter leaving a thick, dark paste called chocolate liquor. At this point, it dries again and is then ground into cocoa powder. Other ingredients such as sugar or milk may be added, and the chocolate will be further refined. Before the chocolate is packaged for sale, it is conched for 12 to 72 hours. Conching refers to the process of blending heated chocolate using slowly rotating blades to remove additional moisture and volatile acids.

Chocolate is marketed as **unsweetened, bittersweet, semisweet, sweet, and milk chocolate. Milk chocolate must have at least 12% milk solids** (in the form of dry milk) **and 10% chocolate liquor.** Companies usually offer more than one kind in any of these categories.

Semisweet chocolate — Throughout this book, I have used Callebaut Dark Chocolate discs, or callets, which are 54% cocoa butter. Although they may look like chocolate chips, they are not. In recipes calling for chocolate chips, use those. There are chocolates with a much higher cocoa butter percentage, but using them may alter the outcome of the recipes. Trader Joe's has a great dark chocolate called Pound Plus, it is a Fair Trade Organic Belgian chocolate. The bar is a bit over 17 ounces and very well priced. I use that also. Dark chocolate can be unsweetened, bittersweet, or semisweet.

Milk chocolate — I use Trader Joe's Pound Plus Belgian Milk Chocolate bar which is also a bit over 17 ounces. The only problem with this bar is that I eat too much of it on my own.

White chocolate is not actually chocolate. It is a blend of cocoa butter, sugar, milk solids, lecithin, and vanilla or vanillin. It is important to read the label. If it doesn't contain cocoa butter, it is confectionary coating, or summer coating, which isn't the same product. Extreme care must be taken when melting white chocolate. It is particularly prone to seizing, or clumping. It is best to place it over barely simmering water until most of it is melted. Remove from the heat and whisk gently to melt the remainder. Adding shortening or cocoa butter to seized chocolate can return it to a liquid state, but it may or may not work in the recipe.

Melting chocolate – Although I have read about melting chocolate in the microwave at full power, I prefer the safer method of melting it at half power — about 2 to 2½ minutes for 3 ounces. It can also be melted in a double boiler over barely simmering water.

Adding liquid to chocolate — Because there is no water in melted chocolate, adding too little liquid can cause it to seize when the liquid is absorbed by the sugar and cocoa, creating solid clumps. To avoid this, it is important to use at least ¼ cup, or more, liquid per 6 ounces of chocolate.

When **liquefying chocolate by itself**, it is important to keep it from getting too hot and keep any moisture from reaching it, as the chocolate can seize. (See definition above). If this happens, you can add vegetable shortening or cocoa butter, a little at a time, to return it to a liquid consistency. Keep the heat low or remove from the heat source completely.

Quick tempering chocolate — A quick version of tempered chocolate can be made using chocolate and shortening in measurements according to the recipe. In a small bowl, melt the chocolate and shortening together in the microwave at half power. Whisk gently to combine and smooth. Do not use oil or butter because they won't harden as the shortening does.

Chocolate chips come in large, regular, and mini. All have their uses. Even when baked, the chips retain their shape. I prefer to use chocolate chips in my cookies so they don't melt all over my hands like chopped chocolate does.

Chocolate sprinkles — This is one place I come down on using only the very best product…Buy the best chocolate sprinkles available! Grocery store "jimmies" are made with cocoa and don't have the chocolate flavor. There are several brands made with real chocolate including **Vermicelli by Cocoa Barry®** and **Guittard Dark Chocolate Decoratifs®**. The latter is the brand I always use. Both are readily available online.

Cinnamon is a commonly used spice in cooking and baking that is both sweet and savory. It comes in sticks (also called quills), ground to powder form, and oil. Sticks or quills are used whole to flavor liquids to avoid the little specks of cinnamon in the final product. The powdered form is used in every form of cooking and baking. Cinnamon is the inner bark of a tropical evergreen tree. There are a number of species sold as cinnamon. Ceylon, from Sri Lanka, is considered the true cinnamon dating back to Chinese writings from 2800 B.C. It is considered less sweet with a more complex, citrus flavor. There is also Korintje cinnamon, from Indonesia, which has a smooth flavor with less bite. It comes from the southwest coast of Sumatra, where it grows wild on the government-protected slopes of Mount Kerinci. Vietnamese cinnamon and Cassia (Chinese) cinnamon are native to Southeast Asia, especially southern China and Northern Vietnam. These have a strong, spicy-sweet flavor. I use Korintje cinnamon as I did when I had the bakery.

Citric acid provides the most tang to a recipe, especially ones featuring lemon or lime flavor. It is important to buy food grade citric acid.

Citrus zest or rinds add powerful flavor to any cookie. Using a microplane grater to grate the peel will make a drier zest, and will minimize the addition of the bitter white pith underneath the peel.

Cocoa powder is powdered unsweetened chocolate liqueur in its natural form. Cocoa must contain a minimum of 10% cocoa butter; however, a higher range of cocoa butter (between 22% and 24%) produces a richer color and deeper flavor.

If a recipe doesn't specify, either natural or Dutch cocoa can be used; however, which one is used in a recipe can be determined from the specified leavening agent. See below. Cocoa has a tendency to clump and not mix well, so sift the cocoa before adding it to the rest of the ingredients to ensure a smooth batter.

Dutch cocoa, also referred to as European cocoa, has been treated with an alkali to help neutralize the natural acidity of chocolate. When baked, it has a darker color. I use Cocoa Barry Extra Brute Dutch Process cocoa powder which is 22% to 24% cocoa butter fat but there are a number of good brands.

Baking powder should be used as the leavening agent in recipes using Dutch cocoa.

Black cocoa has been more heavily Dutched, meaning treated with alkali, resulting in an even deeper color. This cocoa requires the use of baking powder as the leavening agent. I used Black Onyx cocoa in this book.

Natural cocoa in grocery stores is usually the minimum 10% cocoa butter fat. Since I use little natural cocoa, I usually can find Ghiradelli on my grocer's shelf. Baking soda should be used as the leavening agent with this cocoa.

Cocoa butter is the cream-colored vegetable fat by-product of making chocolate and cocoa powder. It is the main component in white chocolate, and can be used to make seized chocolate whole again by adding a little at a time until it smooths out.

Coconut is used sweetened, unsweetened, and desiccated in these recipes. Desiccated coconut is dried coconut, and can be bought shredded or finely cut. I have used both in this book. They are available in fine cut or longer shreds.

Cornstarch is a powder obtained from the endosperm of the corn kernel. It can be used as a thickener as well as an anti-clumping agent, as in powdered sugar.

Corn syrup is made by mixing cornstarch with acids or enzymes. It is a thick, sweet syrup. It comes in light, which is clear and colorless, and dark, which is almost black and has a very distinct flavor. It deters crystallization when added to sugar syrups and caramel. Dark corn syrup can be made at home by adding 1 tablespoon molasses to 1 cup clear corn syrup.

Cream is the byproduct of non-homogenized milk. Upon standing, the milk separates into two layers, a rich cream on top and skim milk on the bottom. While there are many varieties of cream, the one used in this book is heavy cream, or heavy whipping cream, which refers to the amount of fat in the cream. Heavy cream has at least 36% butterfat and is more stable when whipped. It does not require an additional ingredient to stabilize. To whip, chill the bowl, beaters, and cream. Add the cream, powdered sugar, and flavoring (if called for). Beat on medium speed until it begins to thicken, then turn the speed to high and whip to the desired consistency.

Cream cheese is made from cow's milk, and is an original American cheese developed in 1872. Its spreadable consistency makes it popular in both savory cooking and sweet baking. By law, it must contain a minimum of 33% butterfat and a maximum of 55% moisture. Neufchatel cheese is the lower fat version, with 23% butterfat and less moisture. Low-fat cream cheese can be substituted in most recipes, but not the fat-free variety.

Cream of tartar is an acidic byproduct of making wine. It is primarily used to stabilize beaten egg whites to prevent overbeating while attaining maximum volume. By adding 1 teaspoon of cream of tartar to 1 cup of egg whites, it is almost impossible to overbeat them. Cream of tartar is also used to stop crystallization when making sugar syrups. In a pinch, it can be one of three ingredients used to make baking powder.

Dark rum (see rum)

Dried fruit (see fruit)

Eggs used in baking come from hens, and are graded and sized by the USDA. Eggs are graded AA, A, B, and C in descending order, with the classification being determined by both exterior and interior qualities, with the freshness of the egg as the main criteria. Exterior quality is determined by shape, texture, soundness, and cleanliness. Interior quality is determined by the size of the air cell between the white and shell at the large end of the egg (the smaller the size, the higher the quality and freshness of the egg), the portion and density of the white, and the firmness and defects of the yolk. In fresh eggs, both the white and the yolk stand high. Eggs are sold by their weight per dozen eggs. Each egg does not necessarily weigh the same, but they must total the given amount for the specified size. Jumbo is 30 ounces per dozen, extra large is 27 ounces, large is 24 ounces, medium is 21 ounces, small is 18 ounces, and peewee is 15 ounces.

Large eggs are specified for all recipes in this book. The color of the egg has nothing to do with the quality or taste. The weight of an egg yolk in a large egg is 17 grams or .60 ounces. The weight of the egg white is 32 grams or 1.13 ounces. This is an excellent example of why I prefer working with grams. For those who have figured out that this is 49 grams total, the remaining 9 grams is the egg shell.

When breaking eggs, it is best to break whole eggs into a small bowl and then put each into the mixer or bowl. Although rare, if a bad egg is added to an otherwise good mixture it will have to be pitched.

When separating an egg, a bit of the shell can sometimes find its way into the white. Nothing is more frustrating than chasing it around trying to get rid of it with your fingers. Use the empty shell to scoop up the errant piece.

Figs used in this book are dark Mission Figs. They come dried or moist. I prefer the moist variety because they don't have to be soaked prior to using.

Flavoring agents can be extracts, oils, powders, or emulsions. Most of the recipes in this book use extracts. Extracts are very concentrated flavoring agents that are usually made through evaporation or distillation. The value of extracts lies in the intense flavor that can be added without altering the consistency or adding volume to the product. This book uses only extracts, oils, and powders.

Vanilla is one of the most, if not the most, used flavoring in baking. Both the extract and whole beans (long thin pods) are the byproduct of a vanilla orchid. The whole beans are often slit and the paste within them, consisting of very small seeds, are scraped out and used as the flavoring. After using the whole bean, they may be rinsed, allowed to dry, and reused. The three most used types are:

Bourbon-Madagascar vanilla beans come from Africa and the Indian island of Reunion. These are the most used vanilla bean, the thinnest of the three, and considered to be rich and sweet.

Mexican vanilla beans are thicker with a smooth, rich flavor and come from the state of Veracruz. However, the areas where they once grew in abundance are being replaced by oil fields and orange groves. Mexican vanilla beans can contain an ostensibly toxic substance called coumarin. It is banned by the USDA and in Europe. There is no way to tell which bean contains the toxin and which doesn't, so it is important to buy from reliable sources.

Tahitian vanilla beans are the thickest and darkest of the three beans. They are intensely aromatic with a floral taste. Of the three, it is often the choice of professional chefs. Although I don't use it exclusively, Tahitian vanilla is my personal favorite. It lends a distinct taste to simple items such as ice cream, pastry cream, sauces, and sables. I don't use it in complex recipes or those with very dominant flavors because it gets lost. It is also the most expensive of the vanillas.

A special note about vanilla: I know it is fashionable to call for pure vanilla in everything; however, the cost of pure vanilla has escalated to the point that I no longer believe this is necessary. I use McCormick imitation vanilla whenever a recipe includes a lot of spices, other ingredients, or chocolate. I reserve the use of pure vanilla for shortbread or butter cookies, where there are few ingredients and the flavor will really stand out. You can also simply double the imitation vanilla for a stronger flavor. *Cook's* magazine conducted a blind tasting of different vanillas. The one most chosen for its flavor was McCormick's imitation vanilla.

Vanilla sugar, often used in baking, can be made by burying several vanilla beans in a canister of sugar and letting it sit for a week or so. The beans can be used over and over. Also, whole beans which have been slit and had the paste removed are perfect for making Vanilla Sugar.

Oils are used to flavor products. They are much stronger than extracts or powders. If using an oil to flavor meringues, make sure it is added at the very end, after the meringue is completely whipped. Adding before this step can inhibit the expansion of the egg whites.

Powders – While I don't use commercial powders, I do pulverize freeze-dried fruit to flavor buttercream.

Flour – All-purpose flour, cake flour, and bread flour are the flours used in this book. Although many grains can be made into flour, all flours used in this book, with the exception of gluten-free, come from wheat unless otherwise specified.

The strength of a flour is determined by its gluten or protein count. The higher the protein count, the stronger the flour. Strong flours are used for blending with other flours and for bread.

While most flours on the market are pre-sifted, how they are measured can make a huge difference in the outcome of a recipe. The only sure way of obtaining the correct measurement is to weigh the flour, which is why scales are used in professional settings and highly recommended for home baking. In addition to being more accurate, it is much faster.

While the flours are sifted at the point of origin, shipping and stacking can condense them. So, if a scale is not being used, stir the flour very briefly with a spoon in the bag or canister. Spoon the flour into a dry measuring cup to the point of overflowing, then sweep the excess off with the back of a knife. If a recipe calls for sifted flour, place a cup used for dry measuring on a piece of wax paper, fill a sifter or strainer about half way with flour, and sift into the cup until overflowing. Sweep the excess off with the back of a knife. This should yield the closest measure to a cup of sifted flour that has been weighed. If weighing the flour, measure it first and then sift.

All-purpose flour comes bleached or unbleached, and can be used interchangeably. Flour can be bleached either from aging or using chemicals.

Bread flour is a strong flour and is used in cookies when a chewy quality is desired. Cookies using bread flour usually rest in the refrigerator overnight for best results.

Cake flour is a very soft flour. It must be sifted before or after measuring because it is lumpy and the lumps don't always come out when mixing.

All recipes in this book use flour that has been weighed.

Flour Weights			
Type of flour	Protein per cup	Sifted, Cup Weight	Unsifted, Cup Weight
Bread Flour	12 to 15%	125 grams or 4⅓ oz.	140 grams or 5 oz.
All-Purpose-Flour	10 to 12%	125 grams or 4⅓ oz.	140 grams or 5 oz.
Pastry Flour	8 to 10%	125 grams or 4⅓ oz.	140 grams or 5 oz.
Cake Flour	5 to 8%	100 grams or 3½ oz.	125 grams or 4⅓ oz.

Food coloring comes in liquid, gel, and powdered forms. As its name implies, it is used to color food products. I prefer the gel form because it does not alter consistency or absorb liquid which liquid and powdered can.

Fruit used in this book is **fresh, dried, or freeze-dried**. Make sure to remove the little package of drying agent, or desiccant, in the **freeze-dried fruit** before pulverizing. I mention this because I have forgotten to do this twice, and had to throw the whole mixture away. When buying **dried fruit**, I look for the moistest variety. If it needs to be reconstituted, cover the dried fruit with very hot water and let it sit while preparing the rest of the recipe. Drain and then squeeze the water from the fruit if it is to be used in a dough, or follow the directions given in each recipe. Dried fruit is more easily cut with scissors than with a knife.

Dried Apricots. When reconstituting apricots, **do not cover the pan**. Most dried apricots are treated with sulfur to help retain their color. By leaving the pan uncovered, the sulfur is dispelled into the air and the flavor is enhanced.

Navel oranges are best when zesting or grating the rind of an orange. The skins are thicker, yielding more zest. If using a grater, be sure to take only the orange part and not the bitter white pith underneath.

Fruit jams and preserves – **Jams** consist of fruit and sugar cooked until the fruit is so soft is loses its form. Jams contain no pieces of fruit. They are sometimes set with pectin. **Preserves** are fruit and sugar cooked, sometimes with pectin, but the fruit is left in large to medium sized pieces. Both jams and preserves are used in pastries. The preserves are often pureed in a processor before using for a smoother filling.

Gelatin is an odorless, tasteless, and colorless thickening agent used to set cold liquids. Gelatin is a collagen, a naturally-occurring protein produced from the bones, tendons, and cartilage of various animals. Most commercial gelatin is made from pigskin. As Muslim and Jewish religions forbid the use of this product, there are other gelling agents available for restricted diets including vegetarian. Gelatin comes in a **granular form** of different strengths. It must always be softened or "bloomed" in cold water, then either added to a hot mixture directly or heated to liquefy if adding to a cold mixture. I use powdered gelatin 250 bloom strength. Knox gelatin sold in grocery stores is also fine. Each envelope contains 2 ½ teaspoons, enough to jell 2 cups of liquid or 1½ cups of solids.

Gelatin sheets or gelatin leaf in paper thin sheets come in various strengths. They are soaked in cold water before adding to the product. The color re-fers to the strength of the gelatin: Bronze is 125 to 155 bloom, Silver is 130 bloom, Gold is 190 to 220 bloom, and Platinum is 235 to 265 bloom.

Golden syrup is a thick amber-colored form of inverted sugar syrup that tastes like caramel. It is used in a variety of baking recipes and desserts. It has an appearance similar to honey, and is often used as a substitute for people who do not eat honey. It can also be used as a substitute for corn syrup.

Herbs are the green leaves of the plant, such as rosemary, sage, thyme, oregano, or cilantro. There are some plants, such as coriander, that produce both an herb and a spice. Cilantro is the leaf of the coriander plant while the seed is a spice. Coriander, garlic, and fennel bulbs are all regarded as herbs rather than spices. Herbs grow in temperate to hot regions, and are best used fresh.

Honey is derived from the nectar of flowers gathered by bees. It is a source of food for them when it is cold or when they are unable to get fresh food. It is thick, sweet, and sticky, and is stored in honeycombs. Generally, the darker the color, the more intense the flavor. There are hundreds of kinds of honey flavored by the source of the nectar such as lavender and wildflower. The most common honeys in America are clover, orange blossom, and sage. It is sold in honeycomb form, chunk-style (having parts of the honeycomb inside), and as liquid that has been extracted from the comb. Honey should be stored in a cool, dry place. If it crystallizes, it can be reconstituted by placing it in a microwave-safe container and microwaving for 30 to 40 seconds at full power (depending upon the amount), or by placing the jar in a pan of hot water. Honey is used in both sweet and savory preparations and makes a delicious spread for toast when mixed with butter.

Instant coffee is used as a flavoring agent or to deepen the flavor of chocolate. It is made from heat-dried fresh coffee and must first be dissolved in liquid before adding to other ingredients. Instant espresso is generally too strong but can be substituted at half the amount called for in the recipe.

Liquors and liqueurs are used in some recipes. **Liquor** is simply the common name for any distilled beverage. To become a **liqueur**, a base liquor (i.e. grain spirit, brandy, rum) is sweetened and infused with fruits, flowers, plants, or pure juices to achieve a minimum sugar content of 2.5%. This is what differentiates the two.

Though you will often see flavored liquors, these flavors are added, rather than infused, further separating them from liqueurs. Both categories can be of equal potency, with some liqueurs going as high as 110 proof. Therefore, alcohol percentage is not a distinguishing factor.

If a non-alcoholic version is desired, the liquor or liqueur can be heated to evaporate the alcohol. This will retain the flavor. You may also substitute water, but this will alter the taste.

To avoid buying large bottles, I buy the single-serve "airline" bottles, which contain about ¼ cup.

Milk – Several different kinds of milk are used throughout this book. I have used **2% milk,** but whole milk will also work. What will not work, however, is skim milk. **Condensed milk** and e**vaporated milk** are also used. The two are not the same and should not be substituted one for the other. **Evaporated milk** is heated until about 60% of the water in the milk has evaporated, leaving a thickened unsweetened milk. **Condensed milk** has had some of the water evaporated while held in a vac-

uum. Sugar is added after evaporation. It is ivory in color, thick, and has a faint caramelized taste.

Molasses is a thick, black sweetener made from sugar cane. Grandma's Molasses brand is particularly good because it is refined from the concentrated juice of sugarcane, and bypasses the sulfur used in other brands.

Non-stick baking release sprays do exactly what they imply. They make it possible to get products out of their pans. There are two basic types.

Lecithin based spray uses lecithin as their main ingredient. These are preferred because they have no odor or taste. These sprays often leave a sticky residue on the pans; however, you can avoid this problem by washing them immediately with soap and water.

Oil and flour based spray such as Baker's Joy. This should not be used in gluten-free baking because it contains flour.

Each type is sprayed out of a can, and has its own uses. These sprays are used instead of greasing or greasing and flouring baking pans or parchment paper.

Nuts of all kinds are used throughout this book, both as the star of the recipe and in supporting roles. They are usually toasted to enhance their flavor. I keep nuts in the freezer because they can become rancid quickly in hot weather. If the nuts are going to be used for coating a cookie, I hand cut them for evenness. The processor chops too irregularly and will turn them into powder the more you process. If you decide to use the processor, pulse the nuts and then sift to remove any powdered nuts.

If the nuts have been toasted, it is important to cool them completely before chopping them in a food processor. If they are still warm when processed, they can quickly turn into a paste because of their oil content.

If processing nuts into a powder, process them with a portion of the sugar or flour from the recipe. The sugar or flour will absorb the oil, preventing the nuts from becoming a paste. This will also aid in processing as finely as possible.

When a recipe calls for nuts, it is best to weigh them. Whole nuts measured by volume will yield less than slivered or sliced nuts, simply because they pack down when cut. But, four ounces of nuts is always the same no matter the volume.

Nutella is a sweetened spread containing sugar, oil, hazelnuts, cocoa, and skim milk powder.

Peanut butter is made by crushing peanuts into a smooth paste. It has been used throughout the centuries in various forms. George Washington Carver started the peanut butter craze in America, although that was not his intention. He originally made it to feed hungry children in the South, and to provide them with protein in an easy-to-eat inexpensive form. From there, it became one of the most popular foods in America. It was promoted as a health food at the 1904 World's Fair. Most of us never outgrow our love for peanut butter. Peanut butter comes in both smooth and chunky varieties, and is often enhanced with sugar and/or other sweeteners, vegetable oils, and salt. The peanut butter used in this book is commercial. I use either Jif Creamy or Peter Pan Creamy. Using natural or homemade peanut butter may alter the results in these recipes.

Salt is used to bring out the flavor of ingredients. It is used less in baking than in cooking. It has long been used as a preservative. Much of today's salt is mined from deposits left by dried salt lakes around the world. There are many types of salt including table, kosher, sea, rock, pickling, seasoned, as well as colored salts. While the human body needs salt, too much can be a hindrance to good health. Table salt and sea salt are used in this book.

Shortening as used in this book refers to a white fat that is solid at room temperature, such as Crisco. Shortening is used in some cookies, such as chocolate chip and oatmeal, to prevent them from spreading too much in the oven. Using all butter in these cookies will cause too much spreading.

Sour cream is made from adding lactic acid culture to light cream.

Spices can come from the root, stem, seed fruit, flower, or bark of a tree or plant. For example, cloves are flower buds, cinnamon is bark, ginger is a root, peppercorns are berries, nigella is seed, cumin is a fruit, saffron is stigmas, and cardamom can be used in both pod or seed form. Spices tend to have a stronger flavor than herbs because they are made from the crushed portions of plants that are especially rich in essential oils. However, whole cloves, cinnamon sticks, and star anise can be used to infuse flavor into a liquid, and then removed after flavoring the recipe. Most spices are grown in the tropics and subtropics. They are usually used dried in powder form, and in very small amounts relative to other ingredients. Try to buy spices in small amounts because they lose some of their flavor after they are opened, and continue to deteriorate with time. I keep my most expensive seeds and spices in the freezer where they will last indefinitely.

Sugar refers to a variety of sweeteners most commonly obtained from sugar cane or sugar beets.

Granulated sugar (white sugar) comes in a variety of grinds. It is more coarse than powdered sugar or baker's sugar. It is referred to as caster sugar in England and its present and former colonies.

Powdered sugar, also known as **confectioners' sugar and icing sugar**, is labeled with a number of X's, with the highest number of X's being the finest powder. Simply put, it is granulated sugar that has been ground to a fine powder. A small amount of cornstarch has been added to keep it from clumping up. Powdered sugar dissolves very readily, and is used to make icings. It can be made at home by putting granulated sugar in a blender but not a processor.

Baker's sugar is a superfine granulated sugar that dissolves easily when creaming or making meringue. It can be made at home by putting granulated sugar in a food processor and processing it.

Brown sugar is a granulated sugar to which a varying amount of molasses has been added. Brown sugar comes in light, medium, and dark depending on the amount of molasses added. They can be used interchangeably with little difference. Brown sugar can dry out and become as hard as a brick, but simply microwaving very briefly can soften it again. It can be made at home by adding 1 to 2 tablespoons of molasses per 1 cup of granulated sugar depending on whether making light or dark brown sugar.

Decorating sugars used in this book:

Sanding sugar is a coarse sugar that will not melt in the oven. It glistens and adds crunch to a cookie.

Swedish pearl sugar is found in cake decorating shops, gourmet markets, and on the internet. It is large crystals of very white sugar that will not change when heated. Do not confuse it with Belgian Pearl Sugar whose crystals are too big for most cookies.

Colored sugars are widely available or can be made at home by adding a few drops of food coloring to sugar, putting a lid on the container, and shaking to distribute the color.

Weights are given in grams and ounces. I urge everyone, to the point of obsession, to buy a scale and use it. It is not only faster and easier, but more accurate than measuring by volume and guarantees consistent results every time. No bakery would dream of using anything but scales for measuring. Once you get used to it, there is no going back.

Flour is the most difficult ingredient to measure by volume. Most professionals agree that a cup of all-purpose or bread flour weighs 140 grams or 5 ounces. I am a believer in using gram measurements, as are most professionals, because you don't have partial numbers. 150 grams is 5.33 ounces. When converting, the grams and ounces are rarely equal. They have to be rounded up or down.

So, to summarize, buy a scale and use grams. For your reference: 28.5 grams = 1 ounce. 3 ounces x 28.5 = 85.5 so 85 grams would be used.

Xanthum gum is a food additive commonly added as a thickener or stabilizer. It's used in gluten-free baking to hold ingredients together, which normally would be the gluten's job. It provides the elasticity and fluffiness that gluten gives traditional baked goods. ◆

Techniques

Best Caramel Ever

WHILE THE INGREDIENT AMOUNTS MAY change, the method does not. This is the same caramel we made in huge amounts at the bakery.

There is nothing mysterious or difficult about caramel, but it is very precise. It requires a thermometer that goes to at least 350°F /175°C and a heavy pan at least three times larger than the amount of ingredients.

This is a basic recipe that can be anything from a caramel sauce to a firm caramel candy, all depending on the temperature to which it is taken. For the cookies in this book, the temperature is usually 240°F / 116°C depending on the use; however, take it to the temperature specified in the recipe.

Best Ever Caramel

1   cup water
1¼   cups granulated sugar (250 grams or about
       8¾ ounces)
½   cup corn syrup
4   tablespoons butter (60 grams, 2 ounces, or ½
       stick)
1   cup heavy cream
2   teaspoons vanilla extract

Place the water, sugar, and corn syrup in a 2-quart saucepan.

Stir over heat until the sugar is completely dissolved. Bring to a boil, and wash down the sides of the pan with a natural bristle pastry brush dipped in cold water.

Then, boil without stirring until the mixture becomes a medium golden color.

Take it off the heat, and immediately add the butter and stir until it is melted.

Pour in the cream all at once and stir. Don't worry if some of the cream lumps up.

Clip a thermometer onto the side of the pan if possible.

Return to medium-high heat and bring to a hard boil.

Cook to the correct temperature on a candy thermometer as directed in the recipe. Pour into a container. Do not stir at this point. Allow to cool to room temperature.

This may be made a week ahead and refrigerated. Bring to room temperature to use. If it is still a bit stiff, microwave briefly to soften.

If any caramel is left over, it is wonderful over ice cream or a simple cake, tart, or pie. If it is too stiff to use as a sauce, simply add a bit more cream, heat, and stir together. ◆

Cut-Out Cookies

PLEASE SEE WAX PAPER TECHNIQUE, see page xlii.

In order to cut a sharp edge, the dough must be firm. If it's not, keep the dough on the bottom piece of wax paper and place it on a baking sheet. Chill or freeze until firm. If freezing, make sure it isn't rock hard when it comes out. If it is, allow it to soften slightly. The dough should remain on the bottom piece of wax paper throughout this process.

This simple method will produce cookies with extremely sharp, well-defined shapes that look like they came from the best of bakeries. Freezing the cookies allows them to be transported to baking sheets without stretching out of shape.

If using multiple cutters, place them as close together as possible. Touching is best.

Remove the cutters.

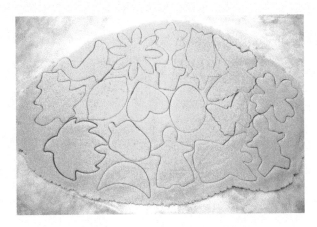

If using a single cutter, place it as close as possible to the previous cutter to get the maximum amount of cookies.

Pick up the wax paper and place the paper with the cut-out cookies on a baking sheet and **freeze until hard**. This will only take a few minutes.

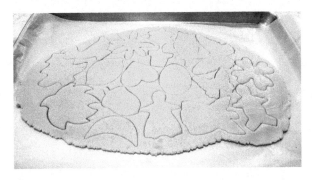

When frozen, go under the cookies with a metal spatula to release.

Push the cookies up through the bottom piece of wax paper and they will pop right out. Alternatively, use a pancake turner to lift them off. If they soften too much at any point, freeze them again.

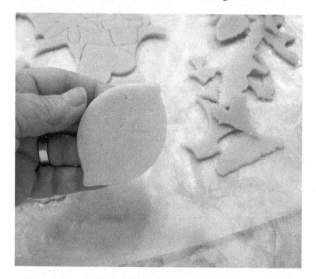

As you remove them, place the cookies on a parchment paper lined baking sheet and bake as directed. I usually let mine soften a bit before baking, especially when finishing with sanding sugar to make sure it can stick to the dough. They can also be baked directly from the freezer, just add a few minutes to the baking time called for in the recipe.

Combine all of the scraps from the first roll-out. Repeat the above steps for more cookies.

Finishes for Cut-Out Cookies

There are multiple ways of finishing these cookies, making them stand-outs on any cookie tray.

Cover the cookies with **sanding sugar before baking**. Finish with one color or several colors at once. There is no need to use any kind of wash on the cookies, the sugar will stick all by itself **as long as the cookie is near room temperature.**

Painted Cookies are absolutely beautiful, and if you finish them with the lemon glaze they are outstanding. See Painted Cookies, see page xxxiv, for how-to photographs.

One of the prettiest and oldest methods of finishing is **stained glass cookies**. Cut out the cookies, then cut a hole in the center. Fill the hole with with hard candy of different colors. Use larger pieces so the colors stay somewhat separate. I blend a mixture of different colors together and then fill with those.

Make sure the hole is filled to the top because the candy will melt and reduce when baked. If you wish to hang these cookies, make a small hole at the top of the cookie with a skewer. When cooled, tie a cord through the hole and hang as desired.

To Double Pan

SOME OF THE RECIPES IN this book include the instruction to **double pan** to avoid overbrowning or nearly burning the bottoms of cookies.

The cookie on the left was baked on a single sheet. The cookie on the right was baked using the double pan technique.

Cookies containing ingredients such as chocolate, cocoa, whole wheat flour, brown sugar, honey, molasses, golden syrup, and corn syrup are particularly prone to overbrowned bottoms before they are completely baked. Double panning prevents this.

To double pan, place the baking sheet with the cookies on top of another baking sheet. This will slow the heat down. By slowing the heat, the bottoms of the cookies will remain the same color as the top.

Because double panning slows down the baking process, additional baking time will be needed. Usually about 10-15% more is sufficient. Simply bake on the middle rung of the oven at the same temperature called for in the recipe.

This technique can be employed anywhere over-browning or near burning is a problem. I use it with laminated dough and any other time I am concerned about possible overbrowning.

I discovered this technique when I wrote my first book, *The New Pastry Cook*. The bottoms of croissants would inevitably burn before they were completely baked. Some time after that, Airbake cookie sheets came out. These consist of two thin sheets of aluminum with air in between. One of the problems with these is water can get between the aluminum layers, making the sheets unusable until the water is removed. Also, the material used in these pans is fairly thin, so I still prefer double panning to ensure the best outcome. ◆

Painted Cookies

MANY YEARS AGO WHEN I first started my bakery, it became abundantly clear to me that I was not a decorator. But in those days, money was scarce so I couldn't hire someone to do it for me. I would see beautifully decorated cookies in magazines and books, and there I sat with really good cookies just waiting for me to devise something.

What I devised was this method of painting cookies. It didn't take long for others to discover it too, and it's still one of the most beautiful finishes for a cookie. The real beauty of this method is that no two cookies ever look alike. They may have the same colors, but the swirling will always be different.

After the cookies are baked and cooled, a powdered sugar glaze consisting of lemon juice or water and an extract for flavoring is made. The glaze has to be thick enough not to run, but thin enough that color can be swirled though. The cookie is dipped into the glaze, any excess runs off, and then it is dried. Any bit that has run down the edge of the cookie can be easily removed.

The glaze will start to become muddied as more and more cookies are dipped. At this point, add more color or start over with another bowl of glaze. It is important to color smaller bowls of glaze for this reason because it can replaced more often. If a lot of cookies are to be glazed, the recipe can be multiplied and held in a large bowl covered with a damp towel to keep the top from forming a skin. When another batch of paint is needed, just add fresh glaze to a clean bowl and start again.

We made thousands and thousands of these in many different shapes, especially for wedding favors and holidays. Sugar cookies or shortbreads are great cookies to use.

Basic Painting Technique
Make sure the glaze is colored in a bowl just large enough to fit the largest cookie and your fingers. You do not want the glaze spread out in a large bowl.

Add dots of color around the perimeter of the bowl and in the middle however you wish. Swirl in a few colors and add more if desired.

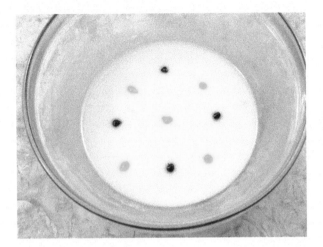

With a bamboo skewer, swirl the colors in a marble-ized fashion.

Lift the cookie and allow the excess glaze to drip back into the bowl. Dripping to one side of the bowl will help keep the paint undiluted as long as possible.

Place the cookie on parchment paper to dry. This can take up to a day if it is humid.

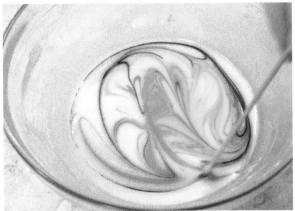

Hold a cookie upside down with the edges of your fingers and dip into the glaze making sure the entire top is covered.

After dipping some cookies, more or different colors may be added and swirled in to freshen the paint.

Dry the cookies completely, making sure they are not just dry to the touch and still wet underneath. After drying, any drips down the sides can be scraped off with a sharp knife. Store in an airtight container with paper between the layers. ◆

Two Press-In Crusts

THERE ARE A COUPLE OF press-in crusts used throughout this book, but the basic technique is the same whether the crust is powdery or a pastry.

Powdery Press-In Crust
Using the amounts specified in the recipe, add the flour to the processor and place the cold butter over the top.

Process until the butter is indistinguishable.

Add the powdered sugar and process until completely mixed in.

Pour the crumbs into the prepared pan. It will look like a lot, that is how it should be.

Distribute the crumbs evenly.

Press in firmly to compact the crumbs into a crust.

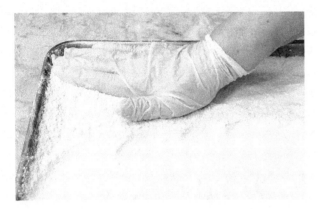

After the crust is firmly pressed in, go around the edges to make sure they are flat and compressed.

Pressed-in crust ready for the oven.

After the crust is baked, it will need to be "spooned." We used this technique at the bakery to secure the crust against the sides of the pan. Because the crust will often shrink slightly from the edges, this will prevent the filling from seeping down into the pan and under the crust. This must be done as soon as the crust comes from the oven. It will not work if the crust is cooled. We found that a soup spoon works well. In the first picture, you can see the crust has slightly shrunk from the sides.

A close-up of the "spooning" technique.

Pastry Press-In Crust

After the dough has been made, remove it from the processor and place in pieces around the bottom of the prepared pan.

Join the pieces by pressing them toward each other.

After all of the dough has been joined, make sure it is evenly pressed in and that there are no seams that can separate during baking.

Press the dough firmly against the sides.

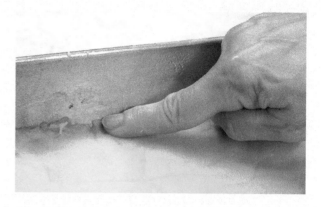

After baking, spoon the crust as below.

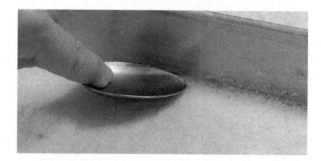

The finished crust.

Flagging or Staggering

Flagging refers to the placement of cookies on a baking sheet. It enables an extra row of cookies to be placed on the sheet, which can be important when baking a lot of cookies.

I learned this method many years ago from an employee and have used it ever since, both at the bakery and at home.

It gets its name from the stars on the flag. Each row is staggered as in the photo below. ◆

Releasing Pan Cookies

SOME BARS AND BROWNIES STICK to their pans no matter what, especially those with a caramel or jam filling. I never liked lining the pans with foil because the foil inevitably wrinkles around the edges. My bakery team and I found a technique that works like magic.

Turn the pan upside down onto a cake board. Hold a blow dryer, set on high, about ¼" away from the edge of the pan. Go around the sides of the pan slowly, and the bars or brownies will drop to the cake board. If they don't, go around again with the blow dryer, or turn the pan right side up and go around the edges with a small metal spatula. ◆

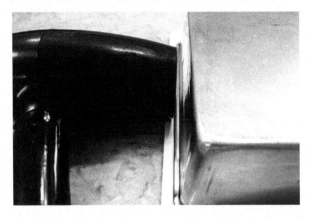

Sifting Ingredients

FOR A LOT OF PEOPLE, seeing the word "sift" in a recipe causes them to think of that clunky triple sifter of the days gone by, like in my mother's day. But, there are ingredients that must be sifted because they won't dissolve when mixed. Some of these ingredients are cake flour, cocoa, and baking soda. All-purpose and bread flours don't need to be sifted because they don't clump up.

Sifting should be done after the ingredients are weighed or measured unless otherwise instructed.

Pictured below is cocoa and cake flour being sifted in a strainer. When clumps of ingredients do not go through, just use a spoon to push them the rest of the way. The important thing is getting them to a powdery consistency, after which they can be whisked together to combine. ◆

Templates

TEMPLATES ARE LIFESAVERS WHEN IT comes to piping cookies to the same size. This is especially useful when the cookies are to be sandwiched.

At the bakery, we made templates in many sizes depending on what we were baking. We saved them so they could be used over and over. Be sure to remember to remove the template before the cookies go into the oven. I'm not sure why I was the only one who had trouble remembering this. In fact, I still do. I always remember just as I close the oven door. I have become amazingly quick at retrieving the cookies and removing the template for the next batch before the heat gets to them.

To Make the Template

Choose a round cutter of whatever size you want the cookies to be. On a piece of parchment paper the size of the baking sheet, use the cutter to trace circles spaced about 1" to 2" apart.

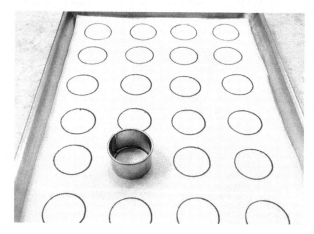

Place the template on the baking sheet and cover with another piece of parchment paper.

If the batter is fairly stiff, pipe the cookies to fill the template. However, as you can see below, loose batter should be piped quite a bit inside the template outline because it will spread to fill.

Remove the template. Place it on another baking sheet and cover with parchment paper to use again for the next batch.

Store the template and use it over and over. Mark the template with the name of the cookie. ◆

"Thumbprint" Cookies

OFTEN REFERRED TO AS THUMBPRINT cookies, these cookies have an indentation in the top where jam, caramel, or some other filling is placed. The Caramel-Filled Chocolate Gems on page 96 are a good example of this type of cookie.

Maybe it's just my thumb, but I have never been successful in using it to make indentations. So, here is a different way of making these cookies.

Roll a small amount of dough into a ball.

Holding it straight up and down, insert the end of a wooden spoon into the center of the ball. It should go almost, but not completely, to the bottom of the cookie.

Widen the hole by rotating the wooden spoon at a slight angle.

Place the finished cookie on a baking sheet.

When baked, the hole will most likely have filled in and expanded in size. If you wish for the hole to be deeper, reshape using the wooden spoon as soon as the cookies come out of the oven. They cannot be reworked once cooled. ◆

Wax Paper Technique For Rolling Out Dough

Rolling dough between wax paper is especially useful for soft or butter-rich dough. This technique allows the dough to be rolled without incorporating additional raw flour, as is done when flouring a surface to prevent dough from sticking.

Another reason to use wax paper is the ease of transferring the dough to the refrigerator or freezer to firm.

Wax paper comes in rolls and can be found on grocery store shelves.

Wax paper is coated with a very thin layer of paraffin. It is water resistant but not heatproof, so it shouldn't be used to line baking sheets and pans. However, it is the perfect vehicle for rolling dough for cut-out cookies or into a certain size. Placing the dough between two sheets of wax paper enables you to see the dough while you are rolling. Is one side too thick or one end too thin? Is the dough wrinkling on the bottom? You can see it all.

Also, because the paper is thin and flexible, simply running your hand over the top piece will allow you to find and correct any uneven spots.

I find wax paper to be very useful for rolling dough to a certain size or shape. Simply draw a pattern on the wax paper with a heavy marker. Make sure the marked side is on top when rolling so it does not touch the dough. You can now see where you need to roll to reach the desired size or shape.

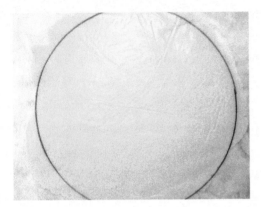

Parchment Paper

While I couldn't bake without this kitchen staple, I never use it for rolling out dough. I find that its strength and thickness makes it difficult to roll dough without excess wrinkling of the paper, and its opacity does not allow you to see how the rolling is going.

Parchment paper is a non-stick chemically treated cellulose-based paper, making it perfect for lining baking sheets and pans to enable easy removal of cookies and bars. It is a durable paper that is heat and water resistant.

To Roll Between Wax Paper

The dough should be of rolling consistency, meaning it is neither too hard nor too soft. If it is very hard from being refrigerated or frozen, rest at room temperature until it softens. The dough needs to be firm, but not hard. If it is really soft, refrigerate to firm. If at any point the dough becomes overly soft

and sticks to the paper, pick up the wax paper with the dough, place it on a baking sheet, and briefly refrigerate or freeze.

I have numbered the steps to make it easy to follow. Don't be put off by the number - The steps go very quickly and will become second nature after repeating a couple of times.

Divide the dough into several portions. It is easier to roll smaller pieces of dough than trying to roll all at once.

Tear off two large pieces of wax paper. I usually use about 20" pieces. It is better to have too much than too little. Position the paper so the long side is vertical, or going away from you.

Place the dough on the bottom piece of paper.

Place the other piece of paper on top of the dough. To make it easier to roll, flatten the dough by indenting it several times with the rolling pin.

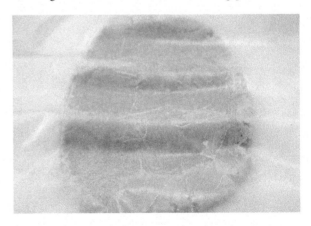

Roll the dough away from you. Turn the paper around so the unrolled portion is at the top.

Roll away from you again. Also roll side to side. I've removed the top piece of paper for the photograph so you can see that the underneath is wrinkling.

Replace the paper and smooth it out. Keeping the dough between the wax paper, flip it over.

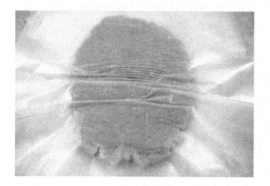

Carefully remove the top piece of wax paper by keeping it very close and parallel to the dough. Dough can stick to the paper if it is pulled straight up, especially if it is soft. Keeping the paper close helps to prevent this.

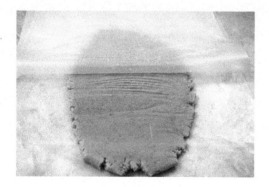

Replace the paper and smooth it out with your hand.

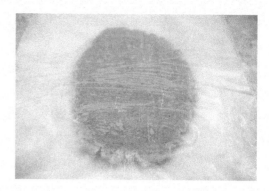

Roll out the dough as before. Flip it over every 3 or 4 times, or whenever you see it wrinkling, remove the paper, smooth it out, and replace it on the dough. This will keep the dough from stalling, which happens when it won't move out any further when rolled. Roll the dough until the desired size or thickness is reached.

The same two pieces of wax paper can be used again as long as there are no tears. In that case, use a new piece of paper.

See Cut-Out Cookies on page xxxi. ◆

Chapter 1
Cut-Out and Sliced Cookies

THERE IS NOTHING MORE WELCOMING than a beautiful cut-out cookie. Often mistaken as coming from the best bakery in town, they are perfect in every form. These beauties can be large, small, rippled, or with sleek smooth edges. They can be made crispy and crunchy, cracker or butter cookie-like, and in myriad shapes and sizes. They add interest to any cookie platter.

Cardamom Black Pepper Snaps

Coconut Macadamia Crisps

Crunchy Pecan Sandies

Painted Sugar Cookies

Lemon Butter Crisps

Chocolate-Dipped Cappuccino Rounds

Limeaways

Chocolate-Dipped Sweet and Salted Butter Cookies

Cardamom Black Pepper Snaps

CARDAMOM IS A FREQUENTLY USED spice in Scandinavian baking, and for very good reason. Its flavor is like no other. While cardamom is not used much in American baking, it should be. Paired with black pepper, while unusual, is delicious. These cookies are very pepper-centric; so if you're not into hot spices, omit the pepper in the sparkly topping.

Because cardamom is so expensive, I store mine in the freezer where it will last forever – or almost!

Cardamom Black Pepper Topping
3   tablespoons sanding sugar
½   teaspoon coarse ground pepper
½   teaspoon cardamom

Mix together in a small bowl. Set aside.

Cardamom Black Pepper Snaps
2   cups all-purpose flour (280 grams or 10 ounces)
1½   teaspoons ground cardamom
½   teaspoon baking soda
½   teaspoon salt
½   teaspoon coarse ground black pepper
6   tablespoons unsalted butter, softened (90 grams or 3 ounces)
1   cup packed light brown sugar (200 grams or 7 ounces)
1   large egg
2   tablespoons coffee liqueur*
     *Or substitute ¾ teaspoon instant coffee in 2 tablespoons water.

Preheat the oven to 350°F / 175°C. Line several baking sheets with parchment paper.

Whisk together the flour, cardamom, baking soda, salt, and black pepper. Set aside.

Place the butter and brown sugar in the bowl of a mixer and beat on medium speed until light. Add the egg and liqueur and beat until combined.

Add the flour mixture on low speed until it comes together. Divide the dough in half (about 325 grams or 11½ ounces each) and refrigerate if too soft to roll.

Roll dough between wax paper to about ⅛" thickness (see wax paper technique, on page xlii). Cut with a 2" cookie cutter or cutter of your choice.

Freeze until hard. Place the cookies on a prepared baking sheet, 4 across and 5 down. Let the cookies thaw on the baking sheets.

Reroll the scraps and continue as above. Sprinkle with the topping.

Bake for 8 to 9 minutes until they are light brown. They will look very puffy and soft, but will flatten and become crisp upon cooling.

Yield: About 36 cookies

Storage: These cookies taste better with a bit of age. They will last a long time in an airtight container. ◆

Coconut Macadamia Crisps

THESE COOKIES FLAUNT A CRISP toasted coconut exterior while hiding a buttery melt-in-your-mouth interior. The interior is graced with toasted macadamia nuts and even more coconut.

Desiccated coconut is used for these. Desiccated coconut is shredded or flaked dried coconut. It can be bought sweetened or unsweetened; and either flaked, shredded, or grated fine, medium, or coarse.

This recipe uses unsweetened small shreds or flakes. If only larger shreds can be found, simply crush them with your hands after toasting. While desiccated coconut used to be an ingredient that was only found in health food stores, it is now much more widely available in regular grocery stores. It can also be labeled as dried coconut.

Coconut Macadamia Crisps

⅓   cup macadamia nuts (45 grams or 1½ ounces)
2   cups unsweetened desiccated coconut (85 grams or 3 ounces)
1   cup all-purpose flour (140 grams or 5 ounces)
¾   cup cake flour (95 grams or 3⅓ ounces)
¾   cup unsalted butter, softened (170 grams, 6 ounces, or 1½ sticks)
¾   cup powdered sugar (100 grams or 3½ ounces)
1   large egg, separated
1   teaspoon coconut extract

Preheat the oven to 350°F / 175°C. Line two baking sheets with parchment paper.

Place the nuts on one of the baking sheets and toast for 8 to 10 minutes if whole, less if they are cut. They will look medium brown and smell fragrant when done. Cool completely.

Spread the coconut in a single layer on the second baking sheet. Be sure to pull any stray pieces into the pile so they don't burn. Toast in the oven for 4 to 5 minutes. They will look golden brown. Stir, and you will see that they are not uniformly browned. Spread the coconut in single layer again, and toast for 2 to 3 minutes until evenly golden brown. Cool. If the coconut was in long strands, crush it between your hands to make small shreds.

Place the cooled nuts in a processor bowl and process to chop coarsely. Add both flours and process until the nuts are indistinguishable.

Place the butter and powdered sugar in the bowl of a mixer. Beat until smooth, then add the egg yolk and extract. Beat until completely mixed. Cover the egg white and refrigerate until needed.

Add ¾ cup (about 60 grams or 2 ounces) of the toasted coconut to this mixture. Reserve the remainder.

Add the flour/nut mixture and beat until everything is incorporated.

Divide the dough into thirds, flatten into discs, and wrap each in plastic wrap. Refrigerate up to 3 days.

Preheat the oven to 325°F / 163°C. Line several baking sheets with parchment paper.

Remove one piece of dough and roll out to about ⅛" between wax paper (see wax paper technique, on page xlii). If the dough is still soft, chill to keep it firm. Cut cookies with a 2" fluted cutter or any cutter of your choice. Place the cookies still on the wax paper on the baking sheet and freeze until hard. This will only take a few minutes as the dough is very thin.

In the meantime, whisk the reserved egg white until foamy.

When the cookies are frozen, remove them with a pancake turner or simply punch them out. Place on the lined baking sheets, 4 across and 5 down.

When the sheet is full, brush the cookies lightly with the whisked egg white. Sprinkle with the reserved toasted coconut, pressing in lightly.

Double pan and bake for 15 to 18 minutes until golden brown. Cool on racks.

Yield: About 60 cookies

Storage: These store well in an airtight container for weeks. They are better made several days ahead. ◆

Crunchy Pecan Sandies

A CLASSIC SOUTHERN FAVORITE UPDATED with the addition of a crunchy Swedish sugar topping. The sugar doesn't melt in the oven, and in addition to adding crunch, it just looks so inviting. A quick drizzle of chocolate completes this classic cookie.

Crunchy Pecan Sandies

1	cup pecans (114 grams or 4 ounces)
1½	cups all-purpose flour (210 grams or 7⅓ ounces)
1	teaspoon cinnamon

½	teaspoon baking powder
½	cup unsalted butter, softened (114 grams, 4 ounces, or 1 stick)
¾	cup powdered sugar (100 grams)
¼	cup packed light or dark brown sugar (50 grams or 1¾ ounces)
2	teaspoons vanilla extract
1	large egg
	Swedish Pearl Sugar as needed
2	ounces semisweet chocolate
1	teaspoon shortening

Preheat the oven to 350°F /175°C. Line several baking sheets with parchment paper. Set aside.

Place the pecans in a single layer on another sheet pan. Toast for about 7 to 9 minutes until they are fragrant and somewhat browned. Cool completely. When they have cooled, pulse them in a food processor to chop them finely. Be careful not to turn them into a powder or paste; the pieces should still be visible. This can also be done by hand. Set aside.

Whisk the flour, cinnamon, and baking powder together. Set aside.

Combine the butter and both sugars in a mixing bowl. Beat until light and fluffy, scraping the sides of the bowl several times.

Add the vanilla and egg, beating until incorporated.

Add the flour mixture, then the toasted nuts, and beat until just combined.

Line a 9x13 inch pan or a quarter sheet pan with foil, letting the long edges of the foil hang over the sides. Press the dough evenly into the pan. Place a piece of wax paper over the dough and run your hand over the top to smooth the uneven spots. Remove the wax paper and sprinkle the dough heavily with the Swedish Pearl sugar. Lightly press the sugar into the dough. Chill until firmly set.

Using the overhanging foil, lift the dough out of the pan. Flatten the sides of the foil so the edges of the dough are exposed. Cut the dough into ¾" to 1" strips crosswise by 2" strips lengthwise. This is easily done with a pizza cutter.

Freeze the dough until hard.

Loosen the dough by gliding a spatula underneath to gently break the cookies apart. Place cookies on the baking sheets with about 1½" between them. Refreeze if they soften too much to break apart.

Bake for 14 to 15 minutes until completely set and firm.

Optional Finish

Combine the chocolate and shortening in a small bowl. Melt in the microwave on half power. Stir together until combined. Dip a spoon into the chocolate and wave airily over the cookies. Allow the chocolate to set.

Yield: 32 to 40 cookies

Storage: Store for about a week in an airtight container with paper between the layers. ◆

Lemon Butter Crisps

NOT ONLY ARE THESE A great tasting cookie, but they can be shaped in three different ways depending on your mood or needs. One of my favorite ways to shape these cookies is using a cookie stamp. I have a set that I got at a craft fair many years ago. Cookie stamps can be found on the internet if there's not a fair in your future.

I have found that there is a difference between the strengths of various lemon extracts. I have made these cookies with both Spice Island Pure Lemon Extract and Penzy's Pure Lemon Extract. Penzy's had a deeper flavor which I prefer for these cookies.

This dough should be worked while it is cool or cold. If it gets soft at any point, refrigerate or freeze to firm and then continue.

Last but not least, these store in an airtight container for almost forever. Not only that, but the flavor

improves as you keep them! Think in terms of the holiday season, when you don't have time to make cookies for yourself or for gifts. These can be made 6 weeks ahead and stored, making cookies readily available for yourself or for giving at a moment's notice.

Lemon Butter Crisps

3	cups all-purpose flour (420 grams or 15 ounces)
1	teaspoon baking powder
¼	teaspoon salt
1	cup unsalted butter, softened (225 grams, 8 ounces, or 2 sticks)
1	cup granulated sugar (200 grams or 7 ounces)
2	large eggs
1	tablespoon lemon zest
1½	teaspoon lemon extract
	Sanding sugar

Preheat the oven to 350°F / 175°C. Line baking sheets with parchment paper and set aside.

Whisk together the flour, baking powder, and salt. Set aside.

Cream the butter and sugar until light. Add the eggs, one at a time, beating until completely combined. Add the lemon zest and lemon extract. Add the flour mixture and mix until completely combined. Refrigerate for several hours to firm the dough.

For Stamped Cookies:

The dough balls must be cold for the stamp to work well. Scoop balls of dough with a #70 disher/scooper, or about 1 tablespoon of dough per cookie. Roll the scoops into balls and roll the balls in sugar. Place the balls about 3" apart on the baking sheets. Press the stamp into sugar, then flatten the balls with the cookie stamp. Carefully remove the stamp.

Refrigerate the cookies before baking to keep them from spreading.

Double pan and bake 22 to 25 minutes until the cookies are light brown in color and browned around the edges.

Cut Out Cookies:

Divide the cold dough into 4 pieces. Work with one piece of dough at a time while keeping the rest refrigerated. Place the dough between sheets of wax paper (see wax paper technique on page xlii), and roll to about ¼" thick. Cut out the cookies as desired.

Refrigerate, or better yet, freeze the cookies until hard. The cookies can be easily lifted with a spatula. The edges will be clean and sharp.

Top with sanding sugar if desired.

Bake as above.

Roll Cookies:

Roll the dough into several logs about 1½" in diameter. Chill or freeze until hard. Slice about ¼" thick and sprinkle with sanding sugar if desired.

Bake as above.

Yield: The number of cookies depends on how they are shaped. The stamped or rolled cookies yield about 40 to 45 cookies. The cut-outs depend on the size and shape of the cutters.

Storage: These will keep for weeks in an airtight container. The logs for the roll cookies can easily be frozen, thawed in the refrigerator, sliced, and then baked. ◆

Painted Sugar Cookies

THIS IS THE IDEAL SUGAR cookie to cut out because it stays flat and keeps its shape. The number of cookies to a recipe depends on the size of the cutters and the thickness of the cookie. For small cookies, roll the dough ⅛" thick. For large cookies, the dough should be rolled to ¼" thickness.

Painting these cookies is a rather messy business. I line my table with parchment paper to minimize the cleanup. Gel colors are best for this technique because liquid colors blend together too quickly. Additional color can be added to the glaze at any time to change the look. Keep in mind that after a bit, the colors will become muddy-looking and fresh glaze will need to be colored.

If making a large batch, double or triple the glaze recipe. Remove a portion and cover the rest with a damp towel. Reportion new glaze as needed.

Sugar Cookies

1   cup unsalted butter, softened (225 grams, 8 ounces, or 2 sticks)

¾   cup granulated sugar (150 grams or 5⅓ ounces)

1   large egg

2   teaspoons vanilla or almond extract, or grated rind from 1 lemon

2½ cups all-purpose flour (350 grams or 12⅓ ounces)

¼   teaspoon salt

Cream the butter and sugar in a mixing bowl until fluffy and very light. Add the egg and beat until completely incorporated. Add the flavoring of your choice.

Combine the flour and salt in a separate bowl and add it to the butter mixture. Mix until everything is well combined.

Divide the dough in half (it will be very soft at this point) and wrap in plastic wrap. Refrigerate for 1 to 2 hours or overnight.

Preheat the oven to 325°F / 163°C. Line several baking sheets with parchment paper. Set aside.

Remove the dough from the refrigerator and roll one piece between wax paper (see wax paper technique, page xlii). It may have to warm up for a few minutes. Cut out the cookies (see page xxxi) and place them on the parchment paper lined baking sheet.

Bake for 10 to 12 minutes if ⅛" thick or 12 to 15 minutes if ¼" thick. No matter the thickness, the cookies should be set and just browning around the edges. Cool completely.

Painted Cookies

Please see page xxxiv of the Technique Section for how-to pictures.

Combine 2 cups powdered sugar and ¼ cup water or lemon juice in a bowl just big enough to hold the largest cookie. Stir with a spoon until completely smooth. Do not use a whisk as it can add air bubbles to the glaze which are hard to remove. Add 1 teaspoon vanilla or almond extract if using water alone.

Dot the surface of the cookie with as few or as many gel food colors as desired. Start with two or three.

With a bamboo skewer or toothpick, swirl the colors around being careful not to over swirl.

Additional color can be added at any time.

Pick the cookies up by the edge and dip, top side down, into the glaze.

Allow the excess glaze to drip back into the bowl.

Place the cookie, top side up, on parchment paper to dry. Repeat this process until the cookies are all glazed or until the color becomes too muddled. The cookies can take up to a day to dry thoroughly depending upon the humidity.

If the glaze has dripped down the sides (it often does), remove it with a sharp knife by gently scraping it away.

Yield: Depends on the size of the cookies

Storage: After the glaze is thoroughly dry, these can be stored in an airtight container stacked with paper between the layers for 10 days or more. ◆

Chocolate-Dipped Cappuccino Rounds

CHOCOLATE, CINNAMON, AND COFFEE! WHAT more is there to say? These cookies are dipped in quick tempered chocolate to avoid streaks or splotches as they sit. If the cookies are to be served over an extended period of time, store the cookies in a container without the glaze, and dip the cookies as needed a day or two ahead.

Cappuccino Rounds

2   ounces unsweetened chocolate (60 grams)

2   cups all-purpose flour (280 grams or 10 ounces)

1   teaspoon cinnamon

¼   teaspoon salt

½   cup shortening (114 grams or 4 ounces)

½   cup unsalted butter, softened (114 grams, 4 ounces, or 1 stick)

½   cup granulated sugar (100 grams or 3½ ounces)

½   cup packed light or dark brown sugar (100 grams or 3½ ounces)

1   tablespoon instant coffee

1   teaspoon water

1   large egg

    Sanding sugar as needed

Preheat the oven to 350°F /175°C. Line baking sheets with parchment paper. Set aside.

Melt the chocolate and set aside to cool.

Combine the flour, cinnamon, and salt. Set aside.

In the bowl of a mixer, combine the shortening and butter. Beat until well combined, then add both sugars and beat until fluffy.

Dissolve the instant coffee in the water. Add the coffee mixture, melted chocolate, and egg to the butter mixture and beat well. Add the flour mixture and beat until completely combined.

Divide the dough in half and roll each half into a 10" log. Roll each log in sanding sugar. Wrap tightly in plastic wrap and refrigerate or freeze.

The logs should be cold, but not frozen, when cut. Cut into ¼" rounds and place on the prepared baking sheets.

Double pan and bake for 8 to 10 minutes. Cool completely.

Quick Tempered Milk Chocolate

8   ounces milk chocolate (225 grams)

2   tablespoons shortening (60 grams)

Melt the chocolate and shortening together in the microwave on half power for about 2 minutes, gently whisking until smooth. Alternatively, melt over a double boiler. Holding the cookie upside-down, dip the top into the chocolate allowing the excess to drip back into the bowl. Place on a rack to dry completely. Or, half dip each cookie and place on parchment or wax paper to dry.

Yield: About 80 cookies

Storage: After the chocolate has set, the cookies can be stored with paper between the layers in an airtight container. These cookies will last for 7 to 10 days.

Make Ahead: Unbaked rolls can be frozen. Thaw in the refrigerator overnight before cutting and continuing with the directions. ◆

Limeaways

THESE DELIGHTFUL LITTLE BITES ADD a bit of surprise to any cookie tray. The lime zest will take you to the tropics on the first bite. Not only are these very easy to make, they should be made at least a week ahead so the flavor can reach its full potential.

Cake flour, being very soft and low in protein, makes a cookie that literally melts in your mouth. However, a warning must go along with these cookies... You may have to hide them before they disappear without ever making it to the cookie tray!

Limeaways
¾ cup unsalted butter, softened (170 grams, 6 ounces, or 1½ sticks)
⅓ cup powdered sugar (45 grams or 1½ ounces)
2 tablespoons lime juice
1 packed tablespoon lime zest from 2 medium size limes
1 teaspoon almond extract
1 teaspoon vanilla extract
2¼ cups cake flour (280 grams or 10 ounces)

Additional powdered sugar as needed

Preheat the oven to 350°F / 175°C. Line several baking sheets with parchment paper and set aside.

Place the butter and ⅓ cup powdered sugar in a mixing bowl. Beat until light and fluffy.

Add the lime juice, zest, and extracts. Beat until light.

Add the flour and mix until completely incorporated.

Divide the dough in half (265 grams or approximately 9 ounces each). Lightly flour the surface and roll each half into an 11" log, about 1¼" in diameter. Wrap in plastic wrap and chill for at least an hour or overnight.

Slice rounds about ¼" thick and place on baking sheets about ½" apart.

Bake for 8 minutes, then turn the pans and bake for another 8 minutes or until just browning on the edges. Cool for 5 minutes or until you can easily pick them up. Be sure that they are still warm, otherwise the powdered sugar will not adhere to the cookies.

In the meantime, sift additional powdered sugar in a bowl. Place the warm cookies by batches in the bowl and gently move them around to coat in the sugar. Gently shake off excess powdered sugar.

Yield: Approximately 88 cookies

Storage: These keep for weeks in an airtight container. If they are stored for several days, coat with powdered sugar again before serving. ◆

Chocolate-Dipped Sweet and Salted Butter Cookies

AT THE RESTAURANT, WE PRESENT these butter cookies, sans chocolate glaze, after the meal has finished. It's just a perfect last bite of something good.

Only recently did I think of adding the chocolate and salted sugar. It takes this cookie to a whole new place and is well worth the extra time. I use Tahitian vanilla because of its unique taste, but any vanilla is good.

Chocolate-Dipped Sweet and Salted Butter Cookies

¾   cup unsalted butter, softened (170 grams, 6 ounces, or 1½ sticks)

½   cup granulated sugar (100 grams or 3½ ounces)

1   large egg yolk

2   teaspoons almond extract

1½   teaspoons vanilla extract, preferably Tahitian

1⅞   cups all-purpose flour (260 grams, 9¼ ounces, or 2 cups minus 2 tablespoons)

Preheat oven to 350°F /175°C. Line several half sheet pans with parchment paper. Set aside.

Cream the butter and sugar until very light. Add the egg yolk and beat until completely combined. Add both extracts and beat well. Add the flour all at once, and mix until the dough comes together in a ball.

If using cookie cutters, divide the dough in half (290 grams or 10 ounces each). If it is too soft to work with, refrigerate for about 30 minutes. Roll between wax paper to about ¼" thickness (see page xlii for wax paper technique) and cut out the cookies. Repeat with the second half of the dough. Gather the pieces that are left over and reroll as necessary.

If rolling and slicing, divide the dough in half as directed above. Roll each half into a 10" log. Wrap in plastic wrap and refrigerate until firm. Slice about ¼" thick.

For either method, place cookies about 1½" apart on the prepared baking sheets.

Bake for 7 minutes, then turn the pan and bake for 6 to 7 more minutes or until lightly browned.

Quick Tempering Chocolate

6   ounces semisweet chocolate, coarsely chopped (170 grams)

1½   tablespoons shortening

½   cup sanding sugar

    Sea salt to taste - I use Baleine Sel de Mer Le sel des Grande Espaces

Melt the chocolate and shortening together. Stir to mix.

Mix the sanding sugar with sea salt to taste. Be careful not to oversalt. You want to be able to taste the salt, but the sugar should be the predominant flavor.

Holding the cookie upside down, dip the top of the cookie into the chocolate. Sprinkle with the sugar/salt mixture. Allow the chocolate to set firmly at room temperature.

Yield: If rolling and slicing, about 70 cookies. If using a cookie cutter, it depends on the size of the cutter.

Storage: After the chocolate is firmly set, the cookies may be stored with paper between the layers in an airtight container for 7 to 10 days.

Make Ahead: The logs may be frozen, thawed, and sliced as needed. Bake as instructed. Dip after baking. ◆

Chapter 2
Drop Cookies

Drop cookies are the most popular cookie of all. And why wouldn't they be? These versatile cookies are the easiest to make. Simply mix the ingredients and drop the cookies from a disher/scooper or by the spoonful. A quick bake in the oven, a brief cooling, and fresh cookies are ready in no time.

Orange Pistachio Delights

Almond Macaroons

Baileys Chocolate Crinkles

Chocolate Snowballs

Peanut Butter Cookies

Vanilla Wafers

Gluten-Free Chocolate Chip Cookies

Chocolate Awesomes

Coconut Mountains

Crispy Crunchy Coconut Crisps

My Oatmeal Cookies

Lemon Crinkles

Mexican Wedding Cookies

Mini Black and White Cookies

My Perfect Chocolate Chip Cookies (with seven variations)

Levain Style Chocolate Chip Cookies

Orange Almond Clouds

Siena Lace

Harlequins

Orange Pistachio Delights

IN MY FILES, I FOUND an orange-flavored cookie from *Midwest* magazine. The cookie was half-dipped in chocolate, and as I read the recipe, more and more ideas started popping into my head. "What if," I thought, "pistachio nuts were added? Or how about mini chocolate chips? Why not roll them in sanding sugar instead of granulated sugar to give them some crunch? What about adding almond extract to go along with the vanilla and orange zest?"

I was feeling pretty good about how this was going. It only took a few minutes to actually make the recipe, and that is where I went off track. I am the first person to emphasize the importance of reading a recipe from start to finish *before* beginning. Well, I didn't follow my own advice; I scooped the first batch, rolled them in sanding sugar, and then into the oven they went.

The cookies featured in the magazine were flat and half-dipped in chocolate. When I looked in the oven, mine were lumpy and anything but flat. So that's when I read further to the part of the recipe where, after you roll the balls in the sugar, they are to be flattened with the bottom of a glass.

The surprise was, they are just as good lumpy and plain as they are flat and half-dipped in chocolate. They are not as pretty, but just as delicious. In the picture above, the cookies in the middle are the lumpy ones.

So make these anyway you wish, just as long as you make them!

Orange Pistachio Delights

2   cups all-purpose flour (280 grams or 10 ounces)
1   teaspoon baking powder
¾   teaspoon salt*
¾   cup unsalted butter, softened (170 grams, 6 ounces, or 1½ sticks)
1   cup granulated sugar (200 grams or 7 ounces)
2   tablespoons orange zest from 2 large oranges
1   teaspoon vanilla extract
1   teaspoon almond extract
1   large egg
⅔   cup pistachio nuts* (75 grams or 2⅔ ounces)
     Sanding sugar as needed

*If using salted pistachio nuts, reduce the salt to ½ teaspoon.

Preheat the oven to 350°F / 175°C. Line several baking sheets with parchment paper.

Whisk together the flour, baking powder, and salt. Set aside.

Combine the butter, sugar, orange zest, vanilla and almond extracts in the bowl of a mixer. Beat until light. Add the egg and mix well.

Mix in the flour mixture on low speed. Add the nuts.

Lumpy Cookies

Pour sanding sugar into a bowl. With a #70 disher/scooper, drop balls of dough into the sugar. Or, use about 1 tablespoon of dough per cookie and roll it into a ball. Roll the balls around in the sugar, pressing it into the cookies. Place the balls on the parchment paper lined baking sheets, 4 across and 6 down, leaving about 2" between them.

Bake for 14 to 16 minutes until browned around the edges.

Flat Cookies

Pour sanding sugar into a bowl. Using a #70 disher/scooper, drop balls of dough into the sugar. Or, use about 1 tablespoon of dough per cookie and roll it into a ball. Roll the balls around in the sugar, pressing it into the cookies. Place on the baking sheet, 3 across and 4 down, at least 3" apart.

Using a flat-bottomed glass cdipped in sugar, flatten the balls to about ¼" thickness. Dip the glass into sugar between cookies. If the glass sticks to the cookies, wipe the bottom of the glass and dip in the sugar again before continuing.

Bake for 10 to 11 minutes until browned around the edges.

Quick Tempered Chocolate

9   ounces semisweet chocolate (255 grams)
4   tablespoons shortening

Melt the chocolate and shortening together either in the microwave at half power or in a double boiler. Pour into a narrow glass or bowl just wide enough to dip the cookies. Dip half of the cookie into the chocolate and place on parchment paper to harden.

Variation: Omit the pistachios and add ⅔ cup mini chocolate chips (114 grams or 4 ounces). Mini chocolate chips are used so the cookies will spread and flatten better.

Yield: About 55 cookies

Storage: Unglazed cookies, either rounded or flat, can be stored for weeks in an airtight container or frozen for several months. After thawing they can be glazed. Glazed cookies can be kept 4 or 5 days in an airtight container. ◆

Almond Macaroons

THESE COOKIES ARE SIMPLICITY ITSELF, and they are one of the easiest, fastest, and most delicious cookies you can make. One of my caterers once said, "I could live on steak and these cookies forever and be happy!"

Be sure to use commercial almond paste, not almond filling or marzipan, for these macaroons. When we needed a large number of these cookies, we made successive batches in the food processor as it does a better job of combining the ingredients into a smooth paste.

I have served these alongside macerated fresh fruit for a lactose- or gluten-free dessert when needed.

Make a template before starting so all of the cookies will be the same size (see page xl).

Almond Macaroons
½   pound almond paste (225 grams or 8 ounces)
⅔   cup sifted powdered sugar (85 grams or 3 ounces)
¼   cup granulated sugar (50 grams or 1¾ ounces)
     Scant ¼ cup egg whites
6   ounces semisweet chocolate (170 grams)
1½   tablespoons shortening

Place the template on a baking sheet. Place a piece of parchment paper on top.

Place the almond paste and both sugars in the bowl of a mixer or food processor fitted with a steel blade. Blend until the mixture is mealy. With the mixer or food processor running, pour egg whites in the and continue mixing until it no longer looks wet. If using a food processor, do not turn the machine off until a ball forms or it is completely mixed as it may stall.

Fit a piping bag with a ⅝" open star tip. Pipe 24 macaroons about the size of a half dollar onto the baking sheet. Let dry for 30 minutes at room temperature.

In the meantime, preheat the oven to 350°F / 175°C. Bake 15 to 18 minutes until a deep golden brown. Cool completely.

Quick Tempered Chocolate
Combine the chocolate and shortening, and melt over a double boiler or in the microwave at half power. Half dip each macaroon into the chocolate and place on wax paper to set for several hours or overnight.

Yield: About 24 cookies

Storage: About a week in an airtight container.

To Make Ahead: The baked cookies may be frozen for several months before dipping in chocolate. Thaw completely on racks, then dip in chocolate.

Note: These may be piped larger or smaller if desired. Use a ¼" or ⅜" open star tip. Dry and bake as above except adjust the amount of time baked depending on the size. ◆

Baileys Chocolate Crinkles

WHAT CAN I SAY? I love crinkle cookies, any crinkle cookie, and these are one of the easiest ones to make. One of the things I like most about these cookies is that they have chocolate instead of cocoa. Additionally, the use of liqueur makes them infinitely versatile depending on the liqueur you use.

The original recipe came from a 1992 *Gourmet* magazine, and it called for Sambuca, an anise-flavored liqueur. But can you imagine these cookies with a coconut, orange, amaretto, crème de menthe, peppermint, Chambord, coffee, or any of a dozen flavors?

Be careful not to overbake these or they will become dry instead of a moist liqueur-flavored chocolate crinkle.

Baileys Chocolate Crinkles

1¼ cups all-purpose flour (175 grams or about 6 ounces)
1 tablespoon baking powder
½ teaspoon salt
12 ounces bittersweet or semisweet chocolate (340 grams)
¼ cup unsalted butter, softened (60 grams, 2 ounces, or 4 tablespoons)
2 large eggs
2 tablespoons granulated sugar (25 grams or scant ounce)
½ cup Bailey's liqueur or liqueur of choice
1 to 2 cups sifted powdered sugar (90 to 180 grams or 3 to 6 ounces)

Whisk the flour, baking powder, and salt together. Set aside.

Melt the chocolate and butter together in the microwave on half power, or place them in a bowl over hot water. Cool to lukewarm temperature.

Beat the eggs and sugar in the bowl of a mixer just to break up the eggs. Add the Baileys or liqueur of choice and mix completely.

Add the melted chocolate, beating well and scraping the sides of the bowl often. Lastly, add the flour, mixing on low speed.

Scrape into a bowl, cover with plastic wrap, and chill overnight.

Preheat the oven to 350°F / 175°C. Line two baking sheets with parchment paper. Set aside.

Sift the powdered sugar into a bowl. Using a #60 disher/scooper, drop a scoop of dough into the powdered sugar. Alternatively, use a heaping tablespoon of dough for each cookie. Roll into balls, coating generously with the powdered sugar. Place about 2" apart on prepared baking sheets.

Bake for 8 to 9 minutes until they are puffy and cracked with soft centers.

Yield: About 30 cookies

Storage: These keep well in an airtight container for a week or longer. Over time, the cookie will absorb the powdered sugar, so it may be necessary to sugar them again. ◆

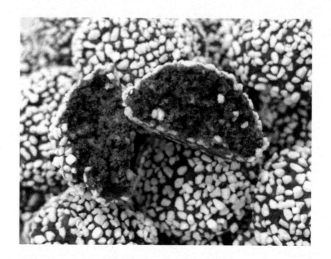

Chocolate Snowballs

THESE ARE VERY INTERESTING COOKIES because they contain no butter, shortening, or oil of any kind. Because they don't have these ingredients to keep them moist, it is very important not to overbake them as they will dry out.

This easy cookie was inspired by the Italians and features orange and lemon zest, cinnamon, cloves, honey, and almonds.

The Swedish pearl sugar contrasts a white crunchy outside with a soft and spicy chocolate inside.

Chocolate Snowballs

1   cup toasted almonds (114 or 4 ounces)
1½ cups all-purpose flour (210 grams or 7⅓ ounces)
½   teaspoon cinnamon
¼   teaspoon cloves
1   teaspoon baking powder
3   tablespoons Dutch cocoa (20 grams or ⅔ ounce)
2   large eggs

½   cup granulated sugar (100 grams or 3½ ounces)

¼   cup honey (85 grams or 3 ounces)

Zest of 1 medium orange

Zest of 1 lemon

1   teaspoon vanilla extract

¼   cup mini chocolate chips (45 grams or 1½ ounce)

Swedish pearl sugar as needed

Preheat the oven to 350°F / 175°C. Line several baking sheets with parchment paper and set aside.

Place the almonds in a food processor along with ¼ cup of the measured flour, and process until finely ground. Whisk these with the remaining flour, cinnamon, cloves, and baking powder. Sift the cocoa over the mixture and blend well. Set aside.

Beat the eggs, sugar, honey, orange and lemon zests, and vanilla extract in the bowl of a mixer until completely combined.

Add the flour mixture and chocolate chips, mixing well. The batter will be very sticky. If it looks wet, stir with a spoon. Cover and let sit at room temperature for 10 to 15 minutes. It will have to set up somewhat, making it easier to scoop.

Place some pearl sugar in a small bowl. Drop several cookies using a #60 disher/scooper into the sugar. Alternatively, use 1 tablespoon of dough per cookie. Turn them over in the sugar to cover the entire cookie. Shape the cookie into a ball by rolling between your hands. Place on the prepared baking sheet, 3 across and 6 down.

Double pan and bake for 10 to 12 minutes. The cookies should be soft to the touch when removed from the oven. Do not overbake or they will be dry.

Cool the cookies completely and store in a covered container. They will develop more flavor if made a day or two in advance.

Yield: 36 cookies

Storage: These last for at least a week in a covered container. ◆

Peanut Butter Cookies

PEANUT BUTTER AND CHOCOLATE CHIP are the quintessential American cookies and are perfect with (or without!) a glass of cold milk.

I have made so many of these cookies that I've lost count. There was a gentleman at my work who would buy at least one cookie a day, and often four to take home to his children. He would see me in the hall and always tell me how good they were. My favorite thing about baking is making people so happy.

Bread flour is used in this cookie because it is stronger and adds to the "chewiness" of the cookie. As with other cookies that contain bread flour, these are best if left in the refrigerator overnight for up to 3 days. They can, however, be baked immediately if needed.

It is important to use commercial peanut butter such as Jif or Peter Pan. Do not use "natural" or homemade peanut butter for this recipe.

Peanut Butter Cookies

2½	cups bread flour (350 grams or 12⅓ ounces)
1	teaspoon baking soda
½	teaspoon salt
1	cup peanut butter (225 grams or 8 ounces)
½	cup unsalted butter, softened (114 grams, 4 ounces, or 1 stick)
½	cup shortening (114 grams or 4 ounces)
¾	cup granulated sugar (150 grams or 5⅓ ounces)
¾	cup packed light or dark brown sugar (150 grams or 5⅓ ounces)
2	teaspoons vanilla extract
2	large eggs
¾	cup salted dry-roasted peanuts (100 grams or 3½ ounces)

Preheat the oven to 350°F /175°C if baking immediately. Line several baking sheets with parchment paper. Set aside.

Whisk the flour, baking soda, and salt together in a bowl. Set aside.

Beat the peanut butter, butter, shortening, sugars, and vanilla in a mixing bowl until well combined. Add the eggs and beat well. It may curdle at some point. If it does, increase the speed of the mixer and continue beating. Adding the flour will solve the problem if beating doesn't. Add the flour mixture and peanuts.

Transfer the dough to a container, cover, and refrigerate overnight. When ready to scoop, allow the dough to sit at room temperature for a while so the dough is easier to shape.

Drop the cookies with a #40 disher/scooper onto the baking sheets. Alternatively, use about 1½ tablespoons of dough per cookie. Roll into balls, place about 3" apart on the baking sheet, and flatten with the heel of your hand to about ½" thick.

Double pan and bake for 13 minutes. Turn the pan and bake for another 5 to 7 minutes. They will look puffy and a little bit wet in the center. They will finish baking on the hot baking sheet. Cool on the baking sheets before removing them.

Yield: About 25 cookies

Storage: Store in an airtight container for 5 to 7 days.

Make Ahead: These can be shaped, flattened, then frozen on a baking sheet. When they are hard, transfer to a freezer bag and store for up to 6 weeks in the freezer. Add a few minutes to the baking time if baking when frozen. ◆

Vanilla Wafers

To this day, I still love the cookies my mother would buy for us as a special treat or when she didn't have time to make something from scratch. Two of my favorites were Sugar Wafers, (chocolate or vanilla, but not strawberry) and Vanilla Wafers. For my blog, I made these Vanilla Wafers to use with the perennial Southern favorite, banana pudding.

In the States, we generally use baking powder or baking soda as chemical leavening agents. But, the baking powder didn't give me the crispness I liked in the store-bought cookies. Then I remembered ammonium carbonate, which is a popular leavening agent in Europe and the Middle East.

Be careful not to smell it when it is opened. It is the same ingredient used in smelling salts to wake people up if they have fainted. The cookies have no hint of it either by smell or taste, although there may be a faint odor while baking. For more information, see page xvii.

Always make sure to buy food-grade ammonium carbonate. Also, take note that the directions for mixing are different if using ammonium carbonate or baking powder.

Vanilla Wafers

1¼   cups all-purpose flour (175 grams or 6⅛ ounces)
¼   teaspoon salt
½   cup unsalted butter, softened (114 grams, 4 ounces, or 1 stick)
½   cup granulated sugar (100 grams or 3½ ounces)
1   large egg
½   teaspoon ammonium carbonate **OR** ¾ teaspoon baking powder
2   teaspoons vanilla extract
1   teaspoon almond extract
½   teaspoon lemon extract

Preheat the oven to 350°F /175°C. Line two baking sheets with parchment paper and set aside.

If using ammonium carbonate: Whisk the flour and salt together. Set aside.

Beat the butter and sugar together until very light and fluffy.

Add the egg and beat to combine. The mixture may curdle. Increase the speed of the mixer and continue beating. If the mixture doesn't come together, don't worry, adding the flour will take care of it.

Stir the ammonium carbonate, vanilla, almond, and lemon extracts together. Add to butter mixture all at once and mix to combine.

If using baking powder: Whisk the flour, baking, powder, and salt together. Set aside. Continue as above, adding the flavorings after the egg.

For both versions: Add the flour mixture all at once and beat on low speed until all of the flour is incorporated. The dough will be very thick. With a #100 disher/scooper, drop the cookies about 2" apart on the prepared baking sheets. Alternatively, drop by rounded teaspoons. If the dough is too soft, refrigerate to firm it. Roll the dropped cookies into balls. Flatten slightly with the heel of your hand.

Double pan and bake for 18 to 20 minutes until golden brown and completely set. Cool on racks.

Yield: 46 cookies

Storage: Keep for weeks in an airtight container. ◆

Gluten-Free Chocolate Chip Cookies

THIS IS ONE OF THE recipes of which I am most proud. Most gluten-free flour substitutes are based on rice flour. While this works for other types of baking, I am not a fan of it used in cookies. It always makes the cookie very gritty which is off-putting to me.

So, I went on a hunt to make a gluten-free chocolate chip cookie that didn't require buying a bag of gluten-free flour substitute. After some intense research, and several failures, I finally came up with a flour to use that is not a substitute, but will stand on its own.

This recipe uses almond flour and processed old-fashioned oats. There are two other unusual ingredients: A bit of cream cheese and xanthum gum, which binds ingredients together in a gluten-free world. It should not be omitted. Xanthum gum can sometimes be found in small packets in stores that feature a lot of gluten-free products. If you're only making these occasionally, that would be your best bet. It can also be bought online in larger quantities.

These cookies have the most interesting texture. Coming from the oven, they are crisp around the edges with a soft middle. But, if you let them stand uncovered overnight, they are a marvelously soft cookie all the way through.

Gluten-Free Chocolate Chip Cookies

2⅓   cups almond flour (200 grams or 7 ounces)

1½   cups ground old-fashioned oats (160 grams or 5⅔ ounces)*

1   teaspoon xanthum gum

1   teaspoon baking soda

1   teaspoon salt

6   tablespoons unsalted butter, softened (90 grams or 3 ounces)

6   tablespoons shortening (90 grams or 3 ounces)

2   ounces cream cheese, softened (60 grams)

¾   cup packed light or dark brown sugar (150 grams or 5¼ ounces)

¾   cup granulated sugar (150 grams or 5¼ ounces

2   teaspoons vanilla extract

2   large egg yolks

2¼   cups chocolate chips (370 grams or 13 ounces)

*The oats must be ground in a processor to a fine powder before using. If measuring by volume instead of weight, measure the oats **after** they have been processed to obtain the correct amount.

1¾ cups unprocessed oats will yield about 1½ cups after processing.

After processing the oats, add the almond flour and process together briefly.

Whisk the almond flour, ground oats, xanthum gum, baking soda, and salt together. Set aside.

Cream the butter, shortening, cream cheese, both sugars, and vanilla until light. Add the egg yolks, mixing in completely. Add the flour mixture. Near the end of mixing, add the chocolate chips.

Refrigerate a minimum of 4 hours, or preferably overnight. The dough can be held for up to 3 days.

Preheat the oven to 350°F / 175°C. Line several baking sheets with parchment paper.

Drop the cookies with a #40 disher/scooper 3 across and 4 down on the prepared baking sheets. Alternatively, use about 1½ tablespoons of dough per cookie. These cookies will not flatten in the oven if they are left as dropped. Flatten to about 2½" with a pancake turner. Don't overdo the flattening. They will resemble hockey pucks with chocolate chips.

However, after flattening, the baked cookie is perfect.

If cold from the refrigerator, **double pan** and bake for 13 to 14 minutes until golden around the edges with the center not quite set. Remove the bottom pan immediately and cool the cookies on the top pan. For crisp cookies, bake another minute or two until completely set.

The cookies can be dropped, flattened, and frozen. If baked from the frozen state, **double pan** and bake for about 15 to 18 minutes.

Yield: About 42 cookies

Storage: Keep for about 5 days in an airtight container. ♦

Chocolate Awesomes

THESE ARE SO EASY THAT you only need a few measured ingredients, a whisk and a bowl. That's it. I even had my grandson make these for my blog.

This type of cookie was everywhere during the '90s. While the names varied, they almost always had Death, Sin, Ultimate, or Decadent in the title, something on the dark or racy theme.

While this is based on the Baker's "Death by Chocolate" recipe, I have an optional ingredient that adds a depth of flavor not found in theirs. Hot chiles and chocolate are a natural and exciting taste combination, so I have added some cayenne pepper to these cookies. If you're not in for adventure or if the cookies are for children, the pepper can be omitted.

These cookies are large but can be made smaller if you wish. Just remember to reduce the baking time by a few minutes as they should remain almost gooey inside.

Chocolate Awesomes

½	cup all-purpose flour (70 grams or 2½ ounces)
¼	teaspoon baking powder
¼	teaspoon salt
⅛	to ¼ teaspoon cayenne pepper, optional
8	ounces semisweet chocolate, coarsely chopped, divided (225 grams)
4	tablespoons unsalted butter, softened (60 grams, 2 ounces, or ½ stick)
¾	cup packed light or dark brown sugar (150 grams or 5¼ ounces)
2	large eggs
1	teaspoon vanilla extract
2	cups walnuts, coarsely chopped (225 grams or 8 ounces)

Preheat the oven to 350°F / 175°C. Line two baking sheets with parchment paper.

Whisk together the flour, baking powder, salt, and cayenne if using. Set aside.

Microwave 4 ounces (114 grams) of the chocolate and all of the butter at half power to melt. Alternatively, melt in the top of a double boiler.

Whisk the brown sugar into the melted chocolate, followed by the eggs and vanilla. When they are well mixed, add the flour mixture. Finally, stir in the remaining chocolate and walnuts.

With a #16 disher/scooper or a ¼ cup measure, drop the cookies on the baking sheets 3" apart.

Double pan, place in the middle of the oven, and bake for 12 to 13 minutes. Cool for about 10 minutes and remove to a rack.

Yield: Approximately 24 cookies

Storage: Store for 3 or 4 days in an airtight container.

Make-Ahead: These can be baked ahead and frozen. Thaw on racks. ◆

Coconut Mountains

THESE NATURALLY GLUTEN-FREE COOKIES ARE a better version of Coconut Macaroons. Swapping half of the sweetened coconut for unsweetened coconut creates an amazing difference. Otherwise, they are essentially just a traditional coconut macaroon that ends up looking like a mountain. It is very important to double pan these be-cause the condensed milk burns quickly.

While the volume measurements for the coconuts are the same, the weights are vastly different. This is because the unsweetened coconut is very dry and weighs less than the sweetened coconut. It is important to note that condensed milk and evaporated milk are very different products, so be sure to use condensed milk.

Mixing the coconuts, condensed milk, and vanilla by hand is a messy business. I use a vinyl glove to minimize the stickiness. I have found a spoon to be rather inefficient and time consuming, but feel free to use whatever works for you.

Many coconut macaroons have the bottoms dipped in chocolate. If the chocolate isn't stabilized it makes for sticky eating and messy hands. I love chocolate with my coconut macaroons, so to avoid this problem, I put it on top of the cookie.

Coconut Mountains

2⅓	cups sweetened shredded coconut (200 grams or 7 ounces)
2⅓	cups unsweetened shredded coconut (125 grams or 4½ ounces)
14	ounce can sweetened condensed milk
1	teaspoon vanilla extract
2	large egg whites
1	tablespoon sugar

Preheat the oven to 325°F / 163°C. Line two baking sheets with parchment paper. Set aside.

Combine both types of coconut in a large bowl. Add the condensed milk and vanilla, mixing them completely by hand or with a spoon.

Place the egg whites in a clean mixing bowl and beat until soft peaks form. Add the sugar and continue beating until firm peaks form. Fold the egg whites into the coconut mixture. Because the coconut mixture is so dense, it will take a bit of folding to fully incorporate. Try to be as gentle as possible so the egg whites don't deflate too much.

Using a #40 disher/scooper or a heaping tablespoon, drop a test cookie onto the parchment paper. If there is a lot of liquid that settles at the bottom, add a bit more coconut (either kind) to the mixture to tighten it. Continue dropping the cookies.

Double pan and bake for about 15 minutes. If they are darkening too quickly, tent lightly with foil. Continue baking for 10 to 15 minutes longer until they are set.

Quick Tempered Chocolate
3   ounces semisweet chocolate
1   tablespoon shortening

Melt the chocolate and shortening together in the microwave at half power or over a double boiler. Using a spoon, drop some of the chocolate on top of the cookies allowing it to run down the sides.

Yield: 28 cookies

Storage: Store in an airtight container for 5 to 7 days. ◆

Crispy Crunchy Coconut Cookies

I AM A COCONUT FAN no matter how it is served - sweetened, unsweetened, toasted, raw, and of course, in a piña colada. Toasting coconut greatly multiplies the flavor and these cookies would not be the same without it.

I use ammonium carbonate, or baker's ammonia, as my leavening agent. It is used in European cookies and was the primary leavening agent used in the past. Baking powder and baking soda are used now in modern kitchens, but I think it is missing something. The ammonium carbonate creates a completely different texture. Baking powder or baking soda are often listed as substitutes, but they can't produce the airy, light, crispy, crunchy cookies that literally bake up with air pockets when they rise in the oven.

This is a simple cookie that is simply sensational.

Crispy Crunchy Coconut Crisps

2¼ cups unsweetened coconut (85 grams or 3 ounces)

½ cup unsalted butter, softened (114 grams, 4 ounces, or 1 stick)

½ cup shortening (114 grams or 4 ounces)

½ cup packed brown sugar (100 grams or 3½ ounces)

½ cup granulated sugar (100 grams or 3½ ounces)

1 large egg

1 teaspoon ammonium carbonate

2 teaspoons coconut extract

2 cups all-purpose flour (280 grams or 10 ounces)

Granulated sugar for dipping

Preheat the oven to 325°F / 165°C. Spread the coconut in a single layer on a parchment paper lined baking sheet. Toast for about 5 minutes until medium brown. Stir, and if not uniformly browned, toast for another minute. Set aside to cool.

Line several baking sheets with parchment paper. Set aside.

Cream the butter, shortening, and both sugars until light. Add the egg, and mix until combined.

Dissolve the ammonium carbonate in the coconut extract and mix into the above ingredients.

Add the flour and beat until combined.

Add the toasted coconut and mix thoroughly.

Using a #100 disher/scooper, drop 4 across and 5 down on prepared baking sheets. Alternatively, use about 2 teaspoons of dough per cookie. I roll mine into smooth balls, but it isn't strictly necessary to do so. Dip a flat-bottomed glass in granulated sugar and press down on the balls to flatten them to about 1½" wide. Imprint the cookies with the tines of a fork. Redip the glass and fork in sugar for each cookie.

Bake for 16 to 18 minutes until firm to the touch. Cool on a rack.

Yield: 45 cookies

Storage: These cookies will last for weeks in an airtight container. ◆

Oatmeal Cookies

3	cups Old-Fashioned Quaker Oats* (300 grams or 10½ oz.)
1	cup + 2 tablespoons all-purpose flour (160 grams or 5⅔ ounces)
1	teaspoon baking soda
1	teaspoon baking powder
1	tablespoon cinnamon
¾	teaspoon nutmeg
½	teaspoon cloves
½	teaspoon salt
1¼	cups packed light or dark brown sugar (250 grams or 8¾ ounces)
1	cup granulated sugar (200 grams or 7 ounces)
½	cup unsalted butter, softened (114 grams, 4 ounces, or 1 stick)
½	cup shortening (114 grams or 4 ounces)
2	teaspoons vanilla extract
2	large eggs
1	pound total of chocolate chips, raisins, dried fruit, or nuts in any combination**

*Do not use Quick Oats.

**If using raisins or another dried fruit, soak them in very hot water while preparing the recipe. When ready to add, drain them and squeeze out any excess water.

Preheat the oven to 350°F / 175°C. Line baking sheets with parchment paper and set aside.

Whisk together the oats, flour, baking soda, baking powder, cinnamon, nutmeg, cloves, and salt. Set aside.

Cream the sugars, butter, shortening, and vanilla until light and fluffy. Add the eggs one at a time, beating until combined. Do not worry if the mixture curdles. Add the flour mixture half at a time, beating on low speed until completely combined. Lastly, add the nuts, chips, or add-ins of your choice.

My Oatmeal Cookies

THERE ARE SEVERAL REASONS WHY these cookies do not spread much. Using all butter in a cookie encourages them to spread when baked, but replacing some butter with a little shortening helps to retain their shape.

Another thing that helps with spreading is loading the cookies with chips, nuts, raisins, or other dried fruit of your choice. The less "add ins" you use, the more they will spread. These cookies call for a full pound of whatever you want. I used a half pound each of milk chocolate chips and raisins.

This has been a go-to cookie since I created it in 2013. I'm happy to be able to share it again.

Drop the cookies about 2" apart onto the baking sheets using a #40 disher/scooper or 1½ tablespoons of dough per cookie.

Double pan and bake for 9 minutes. Turn the pan and bake for 8 to 9 minutes more. They should still be puffy when you remove them from the oven. They will drop and finish baking on the baking sheet as they cool. Cool for about 8 to 10 minutes, then remove to a cooling rack with a spatula. Cool completely.

Yield: Approximately 50 3" cookies

Storage: These keep for five to seven days in an airtight container.

Make Ahead: The cookies may be dropped, frozen, and placed in freezer bags for several months. Add a few minutes to the baking time if baking from the frozen state. ◆

Lemon Crinkles

IN THE BAILEYS CRINKLE COOKIE recipe (see page 19), I wrote about how much I love the look of crinkle cookies. These slightly cakey cookies are no exception. They really deliver the lemon taste. This is thanks to an unusual, but highly effective ingredient: Ascorbic acid or Vitamin C. While it can be purchased in powder form under either name, it is just as effective if you simply crush Vitamin C tablets as long as they contain only Vitamin C. The ascorbic acid enhances the taste by adding depth and a bit of sharpness to the lemon zest and extract.

Lemon Crinkles
2   cups all-purpose flour (280 grams or 10 ounces)

2 teaspoons baking powder

1 teaspoon of ascorbic acid or crushed Vitamin C tablets

½ teaspoon salt

⅔ cup unsalted butter, softened (150 grams, 5 ¼ ounces, or 10 tablespoons)

1 cup + 2 tablespoons granulated sugar (225 grams or 8 ounces)

2 tablespoons lemon zest (from about 2 large lemons)

1 large egg

1 large egg yolk

1½ tablespoons lemon juice

¾ teaspoon lemon extract
   Powdered sugar as needed

Preheat the oven to 350°F / 175°C. Line several baking sheets with parchment paper. Set aside.

Whisk the flour, baking powder, ascorbic acid, and salt together. Set aside.

Cream the butter, granulated sugar, and lemon zest until light and fluffy. Add the egg, yolk, lemon juice, and lemon extract. Beat until completely combined. Add the flour mixture and mix well.

If the powdered sugar is lumpy, sift it through a strainer into a bowl. With a #70 disher/scooper or a scant tablespoon, scoop several cookies at a time and drop them into the powdered sugar. Scoop up a cookie along with some powdered sugar and roll it between your hands. Place on a baking sheet 4 across and 5 down or about 2" apart.

Double pan and bake for 11 to 13 minutes. They should be set but still soft. Let them cool in the pans on a rack.

Yield: About 50 cookies

Storage: Store in an airtight container for 4 to 5 days. If stored for a few days, the cookies may need to be dusted with powdered sugar to perk them up. ♦

Mexican Wedding Cookies

MEXICAN WEDDING COOKIES ARE AMONG the easiest cookies to make and eat. They use only butter, flour, a bit of sugar, and toasted pecans, and they literally explode with flavor in your mouth. Oddly enough, I have also seen these called Russian Teacakes. The only problem with that name is that pecans are native to Mexico and Southern America. Perhaps they used walnuts instead. In any case, as the name suggests, these are a celebration cookie! But of course they are delectable at any time of the year.

The use of cake flour instead of all-purpose and powdered sugar instead of granulated is important to the texture of this cookie.

Mexican Wedding Cookies

¾   cup pecans (85 grams or 3 ounces)
1   cup unsalted butter, softened (225 grams, 8 ounces, or 2 sticks)
½   cup powdered sugar (65 grams or 2¼ ounces)
1   teaspoon vanilla extract
2   cups cake flour* (250 grams or 8¾ ounces)
    Powdered sugar for sprinkling

*Cake flour is softer and lighter than all-purpose flour. As such, it weighs less per cup than all-purpose flour. If you have to use all-purpose flour, use 1¾ cup, as it weighs the same as the 2 cups of cake flour.

Preheat the oven to 350°F /175°C. Line two baking sheets with parchment paper. Set aside.

Toast the pecans until they are fragrant and somewhat browned, about 7 to 9 minutes. Cool completely. Coarsely chop them. Set aside.

Combine the butter, powdered sugar, and vanilla in the bowl of a mixer. Beat until the mixture is almost white, scraping the sides of the bowl often.

Mix in the flour, then the toasted nuts. If the dough is too soft to shape, refrigerate until firm.

With a #70 disher/scooper, drop the dough onto the baking sheets about 2" apart. A tablespoon of dough per cookie may also be used. In either case, roll into balls.

Bake for 12 to 15 minutes until just browning on the edges. Cool. Sprinkle heavily with powdered sugar.

Yield: About 40 cookies

Storage: These keep for weeks in an airtight container. They may need to be sprinkled with powdered sugar again after storing for a few days. ◆

Mini Black and White Cookies

THESE BLACK AND WHITE COOKIES are the iconic New York City cookie. When the executive chef of the St. Louis Hyatt Hotel called and asked my bakery to make these, as a Midwesterner, I had no idea what he was talking about. I had never heard of them.

By that time we had computers, so I went online to find a recipe. This recipe is the one we used at the bakery. Truth be told, I have no idea where it came from, or whether I made alterations.

Black and White cookies are not your usual cookie. They are actually domed cakes that are turned upside-down, and iced half in white and half in chocolate. They really sneak up on you. At first, I wasn't too impressed; however, the more we made them, the more I ate them. I eventually did an about-face and I love them to this day.

The original New York City Black and White Cookie is quite large - too large for me. I have made minis instead and prefer that size. While the cookie part is fast to bake, make sure you leave enough time to ice and finish them. They take a bit of time, but are well worth it.

Black and White Cookies

1	cup cake flour (125 grams or 4⅓ ounces)
1¼	cups all-purpose flour (175 grams or 6⅛ ounces)
½	teaspoon baking powder
¼	teaspoon salt
½	cup unsalted butter, softened (114 grams, 4 ounces, or 1 stick)
⅞	cup granulated sugar (175 grams, 6⅛ ounces, or 1 cup minus 2 tablespoons)
2	large eggs
½	cup milk
2	teaspoons vanilla extract*

*I have used half vanilla and half almond or lemon extract. All are good.

Preheat the oven to 300°F /150°C. Line 3 baking sheets with parchment paper and set aside.

Sift the cake flour, all-purpose flour, baking powder, and salt together. Set aside.

Cream the butter and sugar well. It should be very light. Add the eggs one at a time, beating until incorporated after each one.

Add the flour mixture and milk alternately, starting with ⅓ of the flour. Beat on low speed until blended, then add ½ of the milk. When it is combined, repeat ending with the last ⅓ of the flour.

Using a #60 disher/scooper or a slightly rounded tablespoon, drop the cookies about 2" apart, 4 across and 5 down, onto the baking sheet. They will be a bit raggedy-looking coming out of the disher/scooper, but they will smooth out in the oven.

Bake for 10 to 11 minutes. They will be soft and have no color on the top or the bottom. After 5 minutes, remove the parchment paper with the cookies on it to a rack to cool completely before icing.

Finishing

While some recipes make all of the icing at once and divide it, I prefer to make it in two batches so one doesn't thicken while it waits. These are extremely easy to make.

White Icing

2 ¾	cups powdered sugar (360 grams or 12⅔ ounces)
2	tablespoons corn syrup
3	tablespoons water

Sift the powdered sugar to remove any lumps. Combine the corn syrup and water. Pour this mixture into the powdered sugar and stir to combine.

The icing needs to be thick enough to stay on the cookie without making a puddle at the bottom after sitting for a couple of minutes. If it is too thin, add a bit more powdered sugar. If it is too thick, add drops of water to thin it out until you reach the correct consistency.

Turn the cookie upside down so the flat side faces you. With a small metal spatula, ice one half of the cookie. Let it dry for about 15 to 20 minutes before covering the other side with the chocolate icing.

Chocolate Icing

2¼ cups powdered sugar (295 grams or 10⅓ ounces)

¼ cup cocoa, natural or Dutch (25 grams or slightly less than 1 ounce)

2 tablespoons corn syrup

3 tablespoons water

Sift the powdered sugar and cocoa together. Continue as above for the white icing. After the white icing has dried, ice the other half of the cookie and allow to dry.

Yield: 55 cookies

Storage: After the icing has dried completely, store in a closed container with paper between the layers. They will keep well for about 5 days.

Make Ahead: The cookies can be baked and frozen without icing and kept for several months well-wrapped. Thaw on a rack and ice as above. ♦

My Perfect Chocolate Chip Cookie

While perfection is relative, all bakers have their own "perfect" chocolate chip cookie recipe, including me. This is the perfect base recipe for this type of cookie, and anything can be added to change it. I have provided many variations below, but feel free to create your own.

The use of bread flour gives the cookies a chewy quality, but all-purpose flour can be substituted if necessary. Refrigerating the dough overnight allows the cookies to absorb the liquid uniformly and improves the taste. However, they can also be baked immediately.

While some cookies use chopped chocolate, I prefer using chocolate chips as they are specifically formulated not to melt in your hands like chopped chocolate. I also add more chips than normal, because what's the point of having a cookie named for chocolate chips if there aren't a lot of them inside?

The use of shortening, such as Crisco or any solid white shortening, instead of all butter keeps the cookies from spreading and flattening too much.

For an unbelievable treat, make "chipwiches" by sandwiching two cookies with Chocolate Ganache (recipe included below) or ice cream.

The photo is of the Orange Macadamia White Chocolate Chip Cookies listed below.

Chocolate Chip Cookies

2¼   cups bread flour (315 grams or 11 ounces)
1   teaspoon baking soda
1   teaspoon salt
½   cup unsalted butter, softened (114 grams, 4 ounces, or 1 stick)
½   cup shortening (114 grams or 4 ounces)
¾   cup granulated sugar (150 grams or 5⅓ ounces)
¾   cup packed light or dark brown sugar (150 grams or 5⅓ ounces)
2   teaspoons vanilla extract
2   large eggs
2   cups chocolate chips (340 grams or 12 ounces)

Preheat the oven to 350°F /175°C. Line several baking sheets with parchment paper. Set aside.

Whisk the flour, baking soda, and salt together in a bowl. Set aside.

Beat the butter, shortening, both sugars, and vanilla in a mixing bowl until well combined. Add the eggs and beat well. Mix in the flour mixture. Add the chocolate chips or whatever add-ins you prefer. Refrigerate overnight.

Using a #40 disher/scooper or about 1½ tablespoons of dough, drop the cookies onto the baking sheets.

Double pan and bake for 12 to 15 minutes until set around the edges but still puffy in the middle. Cool on the baking sheet just until firm, then move to a rack to finish cooling.

Chocolate Ganache Filling for Chipwiches

½   cup 40% or heavy cream
6   ounces semisweet chocolate (170 grams)
⅛   to ¼ teaspoon cayenne pepper, optional, but very good

Heat the cream until steamy but not boiling. Submerge chocolate under the cream for several minutes. Whisk gently until smooth. Cover directly with plastic wrap and refrigerate. Bring to room temperature or microwave very briefly to soften when ready to sandwich the cookies. Any of these variations can be sandwiched.

Variations for the Chocolate Chip Cookie – Omit the chocolate chips in the recipe above and add the ingredients below as listed for each variation.

Orange Macadamia Chocolate Chip Cookies – (pictured above) Grate the rind of one medium to large orange, and add to the sugar and butter mixture when beating. Combine ½ teaspoon instant coffee with the vanilla, and add with vanilla as directed. Add 1 cup coarsely chopped toasted** macadamia nuts and 1 cup dark, milk, white, or a combination of chocolate chips.

Pecan Cookies – Add 2 cups coarsely chopped toasted** pecans (225 grams or 8 ounces).

Gianduja Cookies – Gianduja is a milk chocolate hazelnut combination from Piedmont, Italy. Use 1 cup coarsely chopped blanched toasted** hazelnuts

(114 grams or 4 ounces) and 1 cup milk chocolate chips (6 ounces or 170 grams).

Lemon Pistachio White Chocolate – Add about 1 tablespoon grated lemon rind, 1 cup toasted** coarsely chopped pistachios (114 grams or 4 ounces), and 1 cup white chocolate chips (6 ounces or 170 grams).

Cranberry Walnut Cookies – Add 1 cup dried cranberries (soften in hot water if hard*) and 1 cup coarsely chopped walnuts (114 grams or 4 ounces). Squeeze the water out of the cranberries before using.

Cherry Almond – Add one cup coarsely chopped dried bing cherries soaked in hot water* and 1 cup coarsely chopped toasted** almonds (114 grams or 4 ounces). Make sure to squeeze the excess water out of the cherries before adding.

Yield: About 45 cookies

Storage: Keep in an airtight container for several days.

Make Ahead: Any of these variations can be shaped, bagged, frozen, and then baked as directed. Add a few minutes to the baking time if baked from the frozen state.

Notes

*To soak the fruit, cover with very hot water. Let sit for about 10 to 15 minutes. Drain well and pat with paper towels so any excess liquid is not added to the batter.

**To toast the nuts, preheat the oven to 350°F / 175°C. Place the nuts in a single layer on a baking sheet. Depending on the type of nut and size, toasting can take from 7 to 12 minutes. The nuts will become fragrant and turn light to medium brown. ◆

Levain Style Chocolate Chip Cookies

THESE LEVAIN STYLE CHOCOLATE CHIP Cookies are a new twist on an old favorite. In 30 years of baking professionally, I thought I'd seen just about every chocolate chip cookie around. This is definitely a new spin from Levain Bakery that took New York City and the internet by storm.

Basically, this 6-ounce monster cookie uses the same ingredients as most chocolate chip cookies, just in different proportions. They are mixed as a normal chocolate chip cookie. One of the things I've learned when working with cookies is the more you load them up with add-ins, the less they spread. So I made my basic chocolate chip cookie, but reduced the flour, omitted the shortening, used half the fat, and way upped the walnuts and chocolate chips. An overabundance of these makes a really large and fat cookie with very little spread that stays gooey, but not under-baked, when done.

I used bread flour as I do in my normal chocolate chip cookie, and then conducted a little test. I baked half of them immediately upon mixing. I shaped the other half into balls, wrapped them in plastic wrap, and refrigerated them overnight to see if they would bake up differently. If you are going to keep them overnight or freeze them to bake later, remember to weigh and wrap before chilling. The dough is much too stiff to shape when cold. There wasn't a huge difference in how they baked.

Definitely **double pan** these or they will overbrown.

This recipe makes 8 cookies – that is not a misprint, it really makes 8 huge, gooey, fat, chocolate chip cookies that are really, really good. They are best eaten the day they are made, preferably when cooled just a bit but still warm. They can always be made smaller, just reduce the baking time.

Levain Style Chocolate Chip Cookies

2	cups bread flour (280 grams or 10 ounces)
1	teaspoon baking soda
1	teaspoon salt
½	cup unsalted butter, softened* (114 grams, 4 ounces, or 1 stick)
¾	cup packed brown sugar (150 grams or 5¼ ounces)
½	cup granulated sugar (100 grams or 3½ ounces)
2	teaspoons vanilla extract
2	large eggs
2½	cups chocolate chips (425 grams or 15 ounces)
2	cups walnuts (225 grams or 8 ounces)**

*The butter should be softened to about 72°F. It should not be overly softened.

**If the nuts are omitted, increase the chocolate chips by 225 grams or 8 ounces.

Preheat the oven to 350°F / 175°C. Line two baking sheets with parchment paper. Set aside.

Whisk the bread flour, baking soda, and salt together. Set aside.

Cream the butter, both sugars, and vanilla together in a mixing bowl. Add the eggs followed by the flour mixture. Add the chocolate chips and then the walnuts, beating long enough to incorporate them completely.

Using a bowl scraper, turn the dough over in the bowl to make sure there are equal amounts of chocolate chips and nuts at the bottom. If not using the scraper, turn the dough from the outer edges into the center to finish mixing.

Weigh 8 pieces, 170 grams or 6 ounces each. Shape them into loose balls, but do not compact them. If baking immediately, place 4 on a tray. If resting overnight, wrap each ball separately in plastic wrap and refrigerate.

If baking immediately, **double pan**, and bake for 18 to 20 minutes until golden and mostly set. They will have a bit of wiggle in the center and that is fine. They'll finish baking on the pan outside of the oven.

If baking from the refrigerator, add several minutes.

Yield: 8 giant cookies

Storage: Keep tightly covered for a couple of days.

Make Ahead: For warm, just baked cookies, freeze dough that has been portioned, shaped, wrapped, and frozen. These can keep for several months. It is best to let them thaw before baking. They can be cold but not frozen. Bake as above. ◆

Orange Almond Clouds

THESE ORANGE ALMOND CLOUDS ARE a light, but intensely flavored, cookie that is not too sweet. They belong to the meringue family, and have just a bit of flour to soften them. These cookies are quick to make and a great way to use extra egg whites. Dropping them with a disher/scooper makes them easy to form.

Orange with almond is one of my favorite flavor combinations. A large amount of orange zest gives a burst of flavor from the very first bite. These are better after sitting for a few days.

It is best to weigh the almonds because whole, slivered, or sliced can yield different weights by volume. Do not process them when hot from toasting or they will turn into a paste.

Orange Almond Clouds

4   ounces, about 1 cup, almonds, toasted (114 grams) - I use slivered.
¾   cup granulated sugar, divided (150 grams or 5⅓ ounces)
¼   cup all-purpose flour (35 grams or about 1¼ ounces)*
     Zest of 2 large oranges

3   large egg whites (100 grams or 3½ ounces)
1   teaspoon almond extract
     Powdered sugar as needed

*To make these gluten-free, substitute almond flour.

Preheat the oven to 350°F / 175°C. Line three baking sheets with parchment paper. Set aside.

Place the almonds on a baking sheet and toast for about 7 to 10 minutes until they are a medium golden brown. Cool completely.

When the nuts have cooled, place them in the bowl of a food processor along with ½ cup sugar (100 grams or 3½ ounces). Process until the nuts are finely ground. Add the flour and orange zest, and process to mix well.

Place the egg whites and almond extract in the bowl of a mixer. Beat until soft peaks form. Very gradually add the remaining ¼ cup sugar (50 grams or 1 ¾ ounces) and beat until medium stiff peaks form.

Fold in the nut mixture.

Drop with a #40 disher/scooper, or about 1½ tablespoons of dough per cookie, spacing about 1½" apart. Dust well with powdered sugar.

Bake one sheet at a time for 14 to 16 minutes until medium brown. Cool completely. Re-dust with powdered sugar if needed.

Yield: About 36 cookies

Storage: These can be stored in an airtight container for up to a week.

Make Ahead: The cookies can be frozen without the final dusting of powdered sugar. Thaw on racks, then add powdered sugar. ◆

Siena Lace

I WAS A TRAVELING BAKING teacher in Iowa when I first encountered lace cookies. The owner of the school at which I was teaching made them as the dessert at a wonderful dinner. She made hers with almonds and sandwiched them with chocolate. I upped the ante a bit, basing my version on the flavors of Panforte di Siena.

The tastes of Europeans expanded when the trade routes to the Orient opened. Spices, which were never known before, were introduced. From this, the Italian delicacy Panforte di Siena, or The Cake of Siena, was divined. With its exotic spices, sugar, and honey, it was eaten only by the very wealthy.

Siena Lace

2	ounces skinned hazelnuts (60 grams)	
2	ounces blanched almonds (60 grams)	
½	cup unsalted butter, softened (114 grams, 4 ounces, or 1 stick)	
½	cup granulated sugar (100 grams or 3½ ounces)	
1	tablespoon all-purpose flour*	
¼	teaspoon salt	
2	teaspoons freshly grated lemon zest	
2	teaspoons freshly grated orange zest	
½	teaspoon cinnamon	
¼	teaspoon nutmeg	
⅛	teaspoon cloves	
2	tablespoons milk	
3½	ounces semisweet chocolate, melted (100 grams)	

*To make these gluten-free, substitute almond flour.

Preheat the oven to 350°F / 175°C. Toast the hazelnuts and almonds for 7 to 8 minutes until golden brown. Cool completely. Finely grind the nuts in the food processor being careful not to turn them into powder or paste. Set aside. Line baking sheets with foil, dull side up.

Melt the butter in a medium saucepan over medium heat. Add the sugar, flour, salt, citrus zests, and spices. Stir until the sugar dissolves, about 3 minutes. Mix in the nuts and milk. Cook until slightly thickened, no longer than 3 minutes. Remove from the heat. Let sit for 5 minutes.

To speed up the process of dropping the cookies and to give a more uniformed appearance, place the batter in a pastry bag fitted with a ¼" plain tip. Pipe cookies no larger than the size of a dime spacing about 4" apart. Do not let the batter become cold or it will be difficult to pipe. Alternatively, drop by a ½ teaspoon onto foil. The batter will spread considerably when baked. Bake until the cookies are a deep medium brown, 8 to 10 minutes.

Let them cool on the foil, then carefully remove with a spatula as they are very fragile. Wipe the foil with a paper towel and use again. Make sure the baking sheets are cooled before placing the next batch of cookies on them. The cookies can be dropped onto foil while waiting to bake if desired. When a cooled baking sheet is available, just place the foil with the dropped cookies onto the sheet. To hurry the cooling, run cold water over the baking sheets.

When the cookies are cool, thinly spread the underside of one cookie with chocolate and sandwich with another cookie. These are also wonderful plain as singular cookies without chocolate.

Variation: Chocolate Almond Lace

Substitute all almonds for the hazelnuts and almonds. Omit the lemon and orange rind as well as all of the spices. Stir 1 teaspoon almond extract into the mixture after cooking. The directions remain the same.

Yield: About 36 sandwiched cookies

Storage: Store in an airtight container for several weeks with or without the chocolate. ◆

Harlequins

A DELICIOUS THREE FLAVORS IN one cookie, these Harlequins are so unusual. This recipe is based on a simple butter cookie that goes together effortlessly. The dough itself is a breeze to work with right out of the mixer, and the cookies are so easy to shape. You can vary the flavors by substituting other powders for the cocoa and strawberry.

To create the strawberry powder, I processed freeze-dried strawberries in a food processor. Be sure to remove the package of desiccant inside. I once failed to do that, and I had to throw away a whole batch when I saw the shreds of paper in the powder! If you process the whole package, store the leftover powder in an airtight container with the desiccant to keep it dry. Trader Joe's has these in addition to other flavors.

It is important to not overbake these or they lose the balance of flavors. The bottoms should be barely browned, and they will have crisp edges with soft centers.

Harlequins

1   cup unsalted butter, softened (225 grams, 8 ounces, or 2 sticks)

1¼   cups granulated sugar (250 grams or 8¾ ounces)

2   teaspoons vanilla extract

1   large egg

2   cups + 3 tablespoons all-purpose flour (300 grams or 10½ ounces)

½   teaspoon baking powder

½   teaspoon salt

¼   teaspoon baking soda

2   tablespoons freeze-dried strawberries or raspberries, powdered

2   tablespoons cocoa*
     Red food coloring, optional**
     Sanding sugar or granulated sugar as needed

*Any cocoa will do, but there are color variations. I use Black cocoa as it gives the darkest color of all the cocoas. Dutch cocoa would be the next darkest, and natural cocoa gives the lightest brown.

**The use of red food coloring is optional but the cookies will look pretty drab without it.

Preheat the oven to 350°F / 175°C. Line two baking sheets with parchment paper and set aside.

Combine the butter, sugar, and vanilla in the bowl of a mixer and beat just to combine. Add the egg and mix until blended.

Whisk together the flour, baking powder, salt, and baking soda. Add to the butter mixture and beat on low speed until everything is incorporated.

Assembly

Divide the dough into 3 parts (about 270 grams or about 9½ ounces each). Return one batch to the mixing bowl and add 2 tablespoons of strawberry powder. After the powder is mixed in, add red food coloring to get a vibrant red. It is important to note that some color will bake out, so it needs to be darker than desired when going into the oven. Remove to a bowl.

Wipe the mixer with a paper towel if needed. It should be clean enough to continue if a bowl scraper was used to remove the dough.

Place a second portion of dough in the mixing bowl and add the cocoa powder. Blend in completely.

It is easiest to scoop each flavor all at once, then put them together. Wash the disher/scooper in between flavors.

Using a #100 disher/scooper, or about 2 teaspoons each, scoop each of the doughs and line them up on a baking sheet. Cover each batch with plastic wrap as you go along so they don't dry out.

Place one of each color before you.

Gently push them together so they are one. Roll between the palms of your hands to form a ball.

Roll the ball in a bowl of sanding sugar and place on a baking sheet. These cookies will spread considerably, so stagger and place 3 across and 5 down.

Bake for 10 to 13 minutes. The white part will barely be brown and they will be slightly soft in the middle. Do not overbake.

Yield: About 26 cookies

Storage: Keep in a covered container at room temperature for 4 to 5 days. ◆

Chapter 3
Meringues

Who would have thought that egg whites, sugar, and flavoring could whip up into crispy, airy delights? Naturally gluten-free, these easy melt-in-your-mouth cookies are good anytime.

Meringue Introduction

MAKING MERINGUES MAY SEEM EASY, but even professionals have trouble sometimes. You would think that it would be difficult to go wrong with so few ingredients, but alas, it happens. Just egg whites, sugar, cream of tartar, flavoring, and sometimes coloring make up these wisps of air that melt on your tongue.

Humidity is one of the biggest problems. Meringue of any kind should be made on dry days only.

Some say that old, room temperature **egg whites** are best, going so far as to put the mixer bowl with the whites in hot water to heat them. Another suggestion I've seen is to use a propane torch to heat the outside of the bowl. Others say that the fresher the whites the better. I haven't found a noticeable difference between these strategies other than that room temperature whites might rise just a bit higher when beaten. Also, cold egg whites beat up with tighter cells which are a bit more stable. I generally use cold egg whites.

The use of an **acid,** such as cream of tartar, lemon juice, or a bit of vinegar, helps to stabilize the whites while beating. When baked, there is no discernible taste of the acid.

Sugar is the key ingredient in meringues and the type of sugar is important. We would use baker's sugar at the bakery, which is granulated sugar that has been very finely ground but not powdered. The fineness of this sugar allows it to dissolve faster and better in the egg whites. It is important that the sugar be completely dissolved before the meringues go into the oven, or undissolved sugar can pop out in odd places. It is difficult to find baker's sugar in less than 50 pound bags. It can sometimes be labeled as superfine sugar, but either way, you can **make it** instead. Simply put granulated sugar in a processor and process until it is finely ground. I think you will be surprised by the texture. Be sure to put the stopper in the processor or the sugar will cloud the air. This can be made ahead and simply stored in a container. It's wonderful for anything requiring sugar.

The **temperature** at which the meringues are baked is also important. Actually, you are drying the cookies, not baking them. They should not color much, if any. Low and slow applies here with 225°F / 107°C for 1½ hours or more being ideal, depending on the size of the cookie. While they may be baked at higher temperatures, this often causes a lot of cracking.

Cracking can be a problem with meringues. While I like my meringues to be crack-free, I don't obsess over it because they are good either way. Making sure the sugar is dissolved is important. When the whites and sugar have been whipped to stiff peaks, take a little of the mixture between your thumb and finger and feel for the sugar. If you can feel undissolved sugar, whip some more at a lower speed. After shaping the meringues, a slow bake in a warm, not hot, oven will help minimize the cracking.

The **standard recipe** of meringue is twice as much sugar as egg whites by weight. For instance, 3 large egg whites weigh about 100 grams. 200 grams of sugar is twice the weight of the egg whites and measures 1 cup. However, I have found that removing 1 to 2 tablespoons of sugar helps to reduce the cracking without affecting the whipped whites. So, **my standard recipe** is 3 large egg whites to 1⅞ cup sugar or 175 grams; however, there are times that this formula may be altered if other ingredients are being added to the mixture.

When to **add flavoring** to the meringues depends on what you are using. If you are using an extract, it can be added to the egg whites in the beginning before the sugar is added, or added after the meringue is beaten. If using an **oil**, it must be added **after** the whites and sugar are completely beaten. **Coloring** should also be added at the end.

The **basic technique for making meringues** consists of beating the egg whites, acid, and extract to the soft peak stage on medium-high in a stand mixer using **a grease-free bowl with the whip attachment.** Add the sugar by tablespoons about every 25 to 30 seconds so that the egg whites do not become overwhelmed and break down. This also gives the sugar a chance to dissolve before more is added. After all the sugar has been added, continue beating on high speed until the meringue is very, very stiff. Test for undissolved sugar between your thumb and finger. If it is perfectly smooth, add the oil or extract (if adding last), and the coloring. If there is any graininess, continue beating until smooth.

Shape the full mixture at once using a piping bag or dropping from a spoon onto parchment paper lined baking sheets leaving about ¾" between the cookies. More uniform meringues can be made using a template. See page xl.

Dry the meringues for about 1½ to 2 hours at 225°F / 107°C depending on the size. Two baking sheets may be dried at a time by spacing them in the oven. If you have extra sheets, let the piped cookies sit at room temperature and dry in the oven after the others are done.

Cool and **store** indefinitely in airtight containers. ◆

Anise Meringues

THESE MERINGUES CAME ABOUT WHEN one of my readers asked if oil flavorings could be used with meringues. She had queried LorAnn oils, and a customer service person told her that she shouldn't. Around that time, I was asked to do a blog on different types of flavorings for baking.

When I went on LorAnn's website, I found a recipe for Peppermint Meringues which, oddly enough, was flavored with peppermint oil. I love using oils for their intense flavor, and LorAnn oils is a great source. In my experimenting, I discovered that the *time* at which you add the oil makes all the difference. Once the egg whites are beaten to stiff peaks, the oil is added with no deleterious effect. The only oil I had on hand was anise oil. I'm not sure I would have used anise oil had anything else been available, but it proved to be a very pleasant surprise, and ultimately became a cookie that I make again and again.

To ensure even sizes when piping, make a template by drawing 1½" circles 1" apart on a sheet of parchment paper. See page xl.

Anise Meringues

4   large egg whites (130 grams or 4½ ounces)
½   cup granulated sugar, preferably baker's sugar (100 grams or 3½ ounces)
¾   cup powdered sugar (100 grams or 3½ ounces)
4   to 5 drops anise oil or oil of your choice*

*1 teaspoon of extract may be substituted for the oil if desired.

Preheat the oven to 225°F / 107°C. Line two baking sheets with parchment paper and set aside.

In the bowl of a mixer fitted with the whisk attachment, beat the whites to the soft peak stage. Gradually add the granulated sugar, followed by the powdered sugar. Beat until stiff peaks form. Add the oil or extract and beat to incorporate.

Fit a pastry bag with a ¾" open star tip. Fill the bag with the meringue. Hold the bag about ½" above the parchment paper, and pipe to fill the circles if using a template (see page xl). If not using a template, pipe about 1" apart. Pull the bag straight up when finished.

Dry in the oven for 1½ to 2 hours. Turn off the oven and leave the meringues inside until it is cold.

To Finish

4   ounces semisweet chocolate (114 grams)
2   teaspoons shortening

Melt the chocolate in a double boiler, or the microwave set at half power for about 1½ minutes. Stir and microwave in short bursts if additional time is needed.

Dip the bottoms of the meringues in chocolate, and place on parchment paper until the chocolate is set.

Yield: About 36 cookies

Storage: Store in an airtight container for ten days to two weeks. Freeze to keep longer. ◆

Café au Lait Meringues

I ENJOY THE SMELL AND flavor of coffee, but only with lots of cream and sugar. I'm mostly a tea drinker, but I love coffee flavored ice cream and desserts. My easy Café au Lait Meringues are two mocha flavored cookies sandwiched with milk chocolate.

How good does that sound? These are so addictive that I'm happy my husband doesn't like anything coffee flavored. I wish I could say that I practiced self-control and ate them for weeks, but alas, they were gone in a flash!

To ensure even sizes when piping, make a template by drawing 1½" circles 1" apart on a sheet of parchment paper. See page xl.

Café au Lait Meringues

1   to 2 teaspoons instant coffee
1   teaspoon vanilla extract
3   large egg whites (100 grams or 3½ ounces)
¼   teaspoon cream of tartar
⅞   cup granulated sugar, preferably baker's sugar (175 grams, 6⅛ ounces, or 1 cup minus 2 tablespoons)
2   ounces milk chocolate (60 grams)

Preheat the oven to 225°F / 107°C. Line baking sheets with parchment paper and set aside.

Dissolve the instant coffee in the vanilla and set aside.

In a grease-free mixing bowl fitted with the whisk attachment, add the egg whites, and cream of tartar. Beat to the soft peak stage. Slowly add the sugar, about 1 tablespoon every 25 or 30 seconds, and beat until stiff peaks form. Add the coffee/vanilla mixture, beating in until incorporated.

Using a template (see page xl) and a pastry bag fitted with a ¼" plain tip, pipe 1¼" rounds of meringue about 1" apart on the baking sheets. They can also be dropped by heaping teaspoons. To flatten the peaks, dip your finger in water and press down lightly.

Dry in the oven for 1½ to 2 hours. Cool completely.

Cut the chocolate into small pieces. Melt at half power in the microwave or over a double boiler. Match the cookies by size. Dip the underside of the top cookie into the chocolate, letting the excess drip back into the bowl. Sandwich the two cookies together.

Yield: About 55 sandwiched cookies

Storage: These keep indefinitely in an airtight container. ◆

Peppermint Meringues

THIS IS MY BASIC RECIPE for meringues that have both flavoring and coloring. The pink hue adds color to any cookie tray; but if you're like me, you can eat these with or without any other cookies.

For a more uniform size, make a template by drawing 1½" circles 1" apart on a sheet of parchment paper. See page xl.

Peppermint Meringues

3	large egg whites (about 100 grams or 3½ ounces)
½	teaspoon cream of tartar
1	teaspoon peppermint extract
⅞	cup granulated sugar, preferably baker's sugar (175 grams, 6⅛ ounces, or 1 cup minus 2 tablespoons)
	Red food coloring as desired

Preheat the oven to 225°F / 107°C. Line several baking sheets with parchment paper and set aside.

In a grease-free mixing bowl fitted with the whisk attachment, combine the egg whites, cream of tartar, and extract. Beat on medium-high to the soft peak stage.

Add the sugar about 1 tablespoon every 25 to 30 seconds until it has all been incorporated. Raise the speed of the mixer to high, and beat until very, very stiff. Take a small amount of the meringue between your thumb and finger and feel for any undissolved sugar. If there is any, mix a bit longer. Add the food coloring at the very end.

Use a template (see page xl) Pipe onto prepared baking sheets about 1" apart using a ⅜" to ½" open star tip or a teaspoon.

Dry for about 1½ hours. Remove from the oven and cool completely.

Yield: It depends on the size, but about 60 cookies piped with a ½" tip.

Storage: These keep indefinitely in an airtight container. ◆

Chapter 4
Shortbread Cookies

SHORTBREAD COOKIES ARE AMONG THE world's favorites. In its simplest form, shortbreads consist of butter, flour, and sugar. That's it! They can be molded, stamped, rolled, cut out, sandwiched, and made sweet or savory. A more versatile cookie can't be found. I've dedicated an entire chapter to these "best of all" cookies.

Introduction to Shortbread

ALL BAKERS AGREE THAT SHORTBREAD is made with lots of butter, some flour, and a little sugar; however, differences appear outside of this basic framework. The British use semolina or corn flour in theirs. The Scots use rice flour. Some people add cornstarch to reduce the gluten in the flour. Then there is the question of sugar – granulated or powdered? Flavorings? Sometimes yes and sometimes no.

Shortbread is one of the easiest cookies to make. The basis of the dough is butter, flour, and sugar. Butter is the distinctive taste of shortbread, which is why there is a minimum amount of sugar. Flavorings such as citrus zests, cocoa and/or chocolate, spices, and nuts can be added to enhance the shortbreads.

European style butter is perfect to intensify the flavor of these simple cookies. If using a mixer, make sure the butter is not overly softened. The softer the butter, the softer the dough. A temperature of 70°F to 72°F (21°C to 22°C) is ideal.

Shortbread dough can be mixed in a processor or stand mixer. One of its best attributes is that it can be immediately rolled between wax paper, cut out, and transferred to a baking sheet with no chilling at any point.

Shortbread cookies can be made thick or thin, pressed into pans or molds, and used as a foundation for other recipes. While I generally prefer a thinner shortbread, there are times the thicker version works well.

Any shortbread will benefit from being baked ahead and held in an airtight container for several days for the flavor to fully develop. They keep indefinitely and ship well.

If cutting a large, baked shortbread, use a serrated knife and a sawing motion to keep it from crumbling any more than necessary.

The origin of the shortbread recipe is attributed to the Scots. Recipes from Scotland often use some rice flour in addition to all-purpose flour. From Historic UK, comes this explanation of shortbread: "Shortbread was an expensive luxury and for ordinary people, shortbread was a special treat reserved just for special occasions such as weddings, Christmas, and New Year. In Shetland, it was traditional to break a decorated shortbread cake over the head of a new bride on the threshold of her new home. The custom of eating shortbread at New Years has its origins in the ancient pagan Yule Cakes which symbolized the sun. In Scotland it is still traditionally offered to "first footers" at New Year."

Mary Queen of Scots has been given credit for popularizing this cookie. She was particularly fond of a form of shortbread called petticoat tails. They were a round shortbread cookie flavored with caraway seeds and cut into triangles. The triangles resemble the shape of fabric pieces used to make petticoats during the reign of Queen Elizabeth 1. Shortbread was also made in individual round biscuits called shortbread rounds and in a rectangular slab, which was cut into thin pieces known as fingers. All of these variations are still made today.

Here are some interesting facts about shortbread according to the English Tea Store:

Bakers classified shortbread as a bread to avoid paying the tax placed on biscuits.

January 6th of each year is National Shortbread Day.

And from British Food: A History comes the history of the name shortbread: "The large amount of butter is what makes **shortbread** short: the term short, when applied to biscuits and pastry, means crumbly, like shortcrust pastry should be. It is the reason why the fat added to biscuits and pastries is **called** shortening."

No longer a treat just for special occasions, these cookies, along with their many variations, can be enjoyed at any time for any reason. ◆

Basic Recipe for Shortbread

THE FOLLOWING RECIPE IS WHAT we used at the bakery for many years. It can be made in a processor or mixer. I have also included a recipe for chocolate shortbread. European style butter has a higher fat content, making it perfect for shortbread. It adds a deeper flavor to this simple cookie.

There are many possible variations with both the dough and the shaping. It is an easy, versatile, and well-loved cookie that should be in everyone's recipe box.

Basic Shortbread

1   cup unsalted butter* (225 grams, 8 ounces, or 2 sticks)
2½   cups all-purpose flour (350 grams or 12¼ ounces)

½   cup granulated sugar (100 grams or 3½ ounces)

*If using a processor, butter needs to be cold. If using a mixer, butter needs to be softened.

Preheat the oven to 350°F / 175°C. Line baking sheets with parchment paper and set aside.

Processor Method: The butter needs to be cut into small pieces. Add the flour to the bowl of a processor. Pulse several times to sift. Place the cold, cut up butter in a circle on top of the flour. Process until the butter is indistinguishable. Add the sugar and process until a ball forms.

It will take some time for the dough to come together. Redistribute the dough in the processor several times to help it along. Using long pulses will help with the mixing. It will form large crumbs that should be poured onto the work surface and kneaded together.

Mixer Method: For this method, the butter needs to be softened. Combine the butter with the sugar in the bowl of a mixer. Beat until light. Add the flour all at once and beat until it comes together to form a solid mass.

Chocolate Shortbread

2   ounces semisweet or bittersweet chocolate (60 grams)
½   teaspoon instant coffee
2   teaspoons vanilla extract
2   cups all-purpose flour (280 grams or 10 ounces)
⅓   cup cocoa (30 grams or 1 ounce)
½   teaspoon cinnamon
1   cup unsalted butter* (225 grams, 8 ounces or 2 sticks)

⅔   cup granulated sugar (130 grams or about 4½ ounces)

*If using a processor, butter needs to be cold. If using a mixer, butter needs to be softened.

Melt the chocolate over a double boiler or at half power in the microwave. Cool until lukewarm.

Dissolve the instant coffee in the vanilla and set aside.

Processor Method: Place the flour, cocoa, and cinnamon in the bowl of a processor. Pulse several times to remove any lumps of cocoa.

Cut the butter into small pieces. Place them on top of the dry ingredients and process until the butter is indistinguishable. Add the melted chocolate and vanilla mixture. Process until a ball comes together, redistributing as needed.

Mixer Method: Using a strainer, sift the flour, cocoa, and cinnamon together to remove any lumps. Whisk the dry ingredients together. Set aside.

Combine the butter and sugar in the bowl of a mixer. Beat until light. Add the melted chocolate and coffee/vanilla mixture, beating until completely combined. Scrape down the sides of the bowl several times.

Add the flour mixture and mix until a ball forms. ◆

Petticoat Shortbread

This Petticoat Shortbread is made in a clay shortbread mold with a beautifully patterned bottom. The dough is simply pressed in and baked. After releasing, the bottom becomes the top to be displayed before cutting.

This can also be made in a 9" quiche pan with a ¾" side and a removable bottom.

Petticoat Shortbread

Basic Recipe for Shortbread, pg 51

Preheat the oven to 350°F / 175°C. Spray the pan well with non-stick baking release, especially if it is clay and imprinted.

Press the dough evenly into the pan. Bake for 35 to 40 minutes until it is a deep golden brown.

Cool completely, then release from the pan.

Yield: Cut into as many pieces as desired.

Storage: These keep indefinitely in an airtight container. ◆

Peppermint Pinwheels

PINWHEEL COOKIES ADD SO MUCH interest to a cookie plate… Their look alone makes them festive! One batch of dough is divided in two parts, and half is tinted red or any color you choose. Simply rolled up and sliced, these are an easy cookie to make.

Peppermint Pinwheels

Basic Recipe for Shortbreads, pg 51
1   teaspoon peppermint extract
     Red food coloring as needed

Divide the dough in half (about 320 grams or 11¼ ounces each).

Place half of the dough back in the mixer or processor. Add the peppermint extract and about ½ teaspoon of red food coloring. Mix or process to obtain a uniform color.

Roll the red dough between wax paper into a 12x16 inch rectangle (see page xlii for the wax paper technique). Set aside. Do not chill.

Repeat with the white dough. Remove the top piece of wax paper from both rectangles. Using the wax paper on the bottom of the white dough, lift the dough and place it, dough side down, on top of the red dough. Roll it up from the 12" side using the paper as an assist. If the dough cracks, just push it together and continue rolling.

Cut the 12" log in half to make two 6" logs. Roll the logs under your hands stretching them gently to 10" to 11". Refrigerate to firm.

Preheat the oven to 350°F / 175°C. Line several baking sheets with parchment paper.

Slice the logs about ¼" thick. Place cookies on the prepared baking sheets about 1" apart. Bake for about 15 minutes until they just begin to brown.

Yield: About 80 cookies

Storage: These will keep indefinitely in an airtight container. They are best if made several days ahead so the flavor can mellow. ◆

Chocolate Shortbread Hearts

THIS IS A VERY CHOCOLATEY shortbread that can be used alone or in combination with other shortbread cookies. The vanilla extract and instant coffee enhance the chocolate by adding to the depth of flavor. Because there is no leavening in the cookies, either natural or Dutch cocoa can be used. I used Dutch for its deeper color.

I have half-dipped the cookies and finished them with chocolate sprinkles, but they are equally as good just half-dipped.

Chocolate Shortbread Hearts

1   recipe Chocolate Shortbread, pg 51
    Chocolate Sprinkles

Preheat the oven to 325°F / 163°C. Line several baking sheets with parchment paper and set aside.

Divide the dough in half. Roll one half between wax paper to about ¼" thickness (see page xlii for wax paper technique). Remove the top piece of wax paper and leave the dough on the bottom piece. With a 2½" heart-shaped cookie cutter, or any size or design desired, cut out the cookies. Leaving the cookies on the paper, transfer to a baking sheet and freeze for about 10 minutes. Remove the cookies to a baking sheet with a pancake turner. Place on prepared baking sheets. Bring the scrap dough together and reroll for more cookies after they come to room temperature.

Double pan and bake for 12 to 14 minutes until set.

Quick Tempered Chocolate

6   ounces semisweet chocolate
2   tablespoons shortening
    Chocolate sprinkles, optional

Melt the chocolate and shortening together over a double boiler or in the microwave at half power. Stir to combine. Half dip the shortbread cookies. If using sprinkles, hold the cookie over the bowl of sprinkles and sprinkle them on to cover the chocolate, letting the excess fall back into the bowl.

Yield: About 40 cookies

Storage: If the cookies are not finished with sprinkles, they can be held in a covered container for about 5 days before the chocolate will go out of temper. If covered with sprinkles, the cookies can be kept for about 10 days. ◆

Double Ginger Shortbread

I WAS REMINDED OF THIS pan in my collection when I saw a recipe appearing on David Lebovitz' blog using the same one. It's a fun way to serve shortbread. If you don't have this particular pan, use an 8x8 inch pan. To serve, cut it in half horizontally and then in 1" pieces vertically. No one will ever know the difference.

This Ginger Shortbread is enhanced with both powdered ginger and crystalized ginger. These should be made days ahead of time for the flavors to mature. I suggest using a mixer instead of a processor for this recipe so the pieces of crystalized ginger don't become too small.

Double Ginger Shortbread

⅓   cup crystalized ginger
2   cups all-purpose flour (280 grams or 10 ounces)
2   teaspoons powdered ginger
1¾   cup unsalted butter, softened (170 grams or 6 ounces or 1½ sticks)
½   cup packed light or dark brown sugar (100 grams or 3½ ounces)
1   tablespoon sanding sugar

Preheat the oven to 350°F / 175°C. Spray the pan well with non-stick baking release. Set aside.

Coarsely chop the ginger and set aside. Combine the flour and powdered ginger. Set aside.

Place the butter and brown sugar in the bowl of a mixer. Beat until very light and fluffy. Add the flour mixture to incorporate, then add the crystalized ginger.

Press the dough into the pan as evenly as possible. Sprinkle with the sanding sugar.

Bake for 30 to 35 minutes or until medium golden brown. Cool completely before releasing from the pan. Cut in the desired number of pieces.

Yield: I usually cut mine into 16 bars, but they can be cut thicker or thinner.

Storage: These keep incredibly well in an airtight container for weeks. ◆

Lemon Poppy Seed Butterflies

THESE LEMON POPPY SEED BUTTERFLIES are perfect as cut-out cookies. They can also be rolled into logs about 1¼" to 1½" in diameter and sliced. To enhance the lemon flavor, I painted these with an intense lemon glaze to achieve the swirled finish.

Lemon Poppy Seed Shortbreads

    Basic Recipe for Shortbread, pg 51
    Zest of 1 large lemon
2   teaspoons poppy seeds

Preheat oven to 350°F / 175°C. Line several baking sheets with parchment paper and set aside.

Add the lemon zest to the butter and sugar mixture when processing or mixing. Add the poppy seeds at the end.

Divide the dough into halves or thirds. Roll each piece between wax paper to a thickness of about ¼" (see page xlii for the wax paper technique). Cut out using the cutter of your choice. I used a 2" butterfly cookie cutter. Leave the cut out cookies between wax paper and freeze for about 10 to 15 minutes until hard.

Simply pop out the cookies and place them on the parchment paper 1" apart.

Repeat this process with the other pieces of dough. Be sure to let the frozen leftover dough come to room temperature before rerolling.

Bake for 10 to 12 minutes until lightly browned. Cool completely.

Lemon Glaze

1½   cups powdered sugar, sifted (185 grams or 6½ ounces)
3   to 4 tablespoons fresh lemon juice
    Gel food coloring

To paint the cookies, see page xxxiv for how-to pictures.

Stir the powdered sugar and 3 tablespoons lemon juice together. The glaze should be thick enough to coat the cookie without running off, but thin enough to spread on its own. Adjust by adding more powdered sugar to thicken or more lemon juice to thin. Use the juice carefully, a little goes a long way. Test a cookie before continuing.

Place dots of gel food coloring around the bowl of glaze and swirl with a skewer. Dip the top of a cookie into the glaze allowing the excess to fall back into the bowl. Place the cookie on parchment paper to dry.

Yield: Depends on the size of the cutter. I got about 45 cookies using my 2" butterfly cutter.

Storage: After the glaze has dried completely, layer cookies with paper in an airtight container. They will keep for weeks. ◆

Shortbread Daisies

THIS IS THE SIMPLEST SHORTBREAD of all. We sold these at the bakery either as is or painted. They were a favorite for weddings when made in the shape of small hearts. There was a mother who would come in a couple of times a week just to treat her little daughter to one, as they were her favorite. It was always such a delight to see her take her first bite. These are a much-loved plain and simple cookie.

Shortbread Daisies

Basic Recipe for Shortbread, pg 51
Nonpareils as needed, optional

Preheat the oven to 350°F / 175°C. Line several baking sheets with parchment paper and set aside.

Divide the dough in half. Roll between sheets of wax paper to a thickness of about ⅓" (see page xlii for the wax paper technique). Cut out the cookies with a 2" cutter. Place the cookies, still on the wax paper, on a baking sheet and freeze until hard. Remove the cookies with a pancake turner or simply pop them out. Place on the prepared baking sheets about 1" apart.

If using the nonpareils, place a ½" to ¾" round cutter in the middle of the cookie before baking. Carefully drop them into the cookie cutter. Remove the cutter.

Bake for 10 to 14 minutes until lightly browned. Cool.

To Paint the Daisies

See the painted glaze technique on page xxxiv

Yield: About 40 cookies

Storage: These will last for weeks in a sealed container. ◆

Hazelnut Shortbread Balls

MOST NUTS CAN BE SUBSTITUTED for the hazelnuts in this recipe – although peanuts might be a stretch. Easily made and easily finished, these keep and ship well.

Hazelnut Shortbread Balls

Basic Recipe for Shortbread, pg 51

1½	cups hazelnuts, finely chopped (170 grams or 6 ounces)
6	ounces semisweet chocolate (170 grams or 6 ounces)
2	tablespoons shortening

Preheat the oven to 350°F / 175°C. Line several baking sheets with parchment paper. Set aside.

Using a #70 disher/scooper or a scant tablespoon, scoop the dough onto the prepared baking sheets. Roll into balls and space 1" apart.

Bake for 18 to 20 minutes until lightly browned. Cool completely before finishing.

Quick Tempered Chocolate

Melt the chocolate and shortening together in the microwave at half power or in a double boiler. Stir to blend completely.

Dip just the top of the cookie into the chocolate, letting the excess drip back into the bowl. Dip the cookie immediately into the nuts. Place on a parchment paper lined baking sheet to set. To set faster, refrigerate briefly.

Yield: 54 balls

Storage: These will keep for weeks in an airtight container. ◆

Nutmeg Baton Shortbreads

ONE SIMPLE ADDITION TO THE basic shortbread recipe turns this into an unbelievably different cookie. If you love eggnog with nutmeg, you will love this cookie. This shortbread is one of the easiest to shape. Any spice can be substituted or several can be used – it's all up to your imagination.

Nutmeg Batons

Basic Recipe for Shortbread, pg 51
1½ teaspoons nutmeg or spice(s) of your choice

Preheat the oven to 350°F / 175°C. Line baking sheets with parchment paper and set aside.

Make the shortbread using either the mixing or processing method. Whisk the nutmeg into the flour before adding.

Shaping

Divide the dough in half (approximately 315 grams or 11 ounces each). Between wax paper, roll into a 6x9 inch rectangle (see page xlii for wax paper technique). Remove the top piece of paper but leave the dough on the bottom piece.

Cut 1" strips across the 9" side. Cross cut the 9" strips into 3" batons. Mark each baton with the tines of a fork 3 times, spacing them equally. Place the cookies 5 across and 4 down on a baking sheet.

Repeat with the second piece of dough.

Bake for 15 to 18 minutes until lightly browned. Cool.

Yield: 54 cookies

Storage: These keep for weeks and weeks in an airtight container. ◆

Black and White Filled Shortbreads

THIS IS AN ELEGANT COOKIE that packs a flavor punch. While these are filled with raspberry jam, any other seedless jam can be used, as well as any buttercream.

Black and White Filled Shortbreads

1 recipe Chocolate Shortbread, pg 51
1 recipe Basic Recipe for Shortbread, pg 51

Preheat oven to 350°F / 175°C. Line several baking sheets with parchment paper and set aside.

Chocolate Dough

Divide the chocolate dough into halves or thirds. Roll one piece at a time between wax paper to about ¼" thickness (see page xlii for wax paper technique). Cut out the cookies with a 2" fluted round cookie cutter. While the cookies are still on the wax paper, place them on a cookie sheet and freeze until hard. Remove the cookies with a pancake turner and place about 1" apart on the prepared baking sheets. Reroll the scraps after bringing them to room temperature.

Double pan and bake for 12 to 14 minutes until firm and just coloring. Cool completely.

Basic Shortbread Dough

Divide dough into halves or thirds and roll each piece between wax paper to a thickness of about ¼" (see page xlii for wax paper technique). Cut out with the same 2" fluted round cookie cutter. Center a ¾" plain cookie cutter on each cookie. Cut out the round. While the cookies are still on the wax paper, place them on a cookie sheet and freeze until hard. Remove the cookies with a pancake turner and push out the center of the cookies. Place the cookies (without the centers) about 1" apart on prepared baking sheets. Reroll the scraps after bringing them to room temperature.

Bake for 12 to 14 minutes until lightly browned and firm. Cool completely.

Filling the Cookies

¾   cup seedless red raspberry jam or another flavor of your choice

      Chocolate Shortbread bottoms

      Basic Shortbread tops

3   ounces semisweet chocolate, melted

With a ¼" plain tip, pipe a small amount of the preserves on the underside of the chocolate cookie. Place the basic cookie on top and gently press down. Drizzle with the chocolate. Allow to dry for a day or so.

Yield: About 60 each of the chocolate and basic cookie or 30 sandwiched cookies

Storage: The cookies themselves can be made weeks ahead and stored in a container, but the sandwiching should be done no more than a day or two ahead of time. ◆

Cheddar Pecan Savory Shortbreads

SAVORY SHORTBREADS ARE ONE OF the best kinds of shortbread. They're perfect with a drink or as a snack. These flew off the shelves when sold in the retail shop. They also make an excellent hostess gift, and can be shipped stacked on top of each other. There are several variations listed below.

Cheddar Pecan Shortbreads

½   cup pecan pieces (60 grams or 2 ounces)

4   ounces extra sharp cheddar cheese* (114 grams)

½   cup unsalted butter** (114 grams, 4 ounces, or 1 stick)

1¼   cups all-purpose flour (175 grams or 6⅛ ounces)

½   teaspoon salt

¼   to ½ teaspoon cayenne pepper

*Use Cabot's Extremely Sharp Cheddar Cheese if available.

**Cold for the processor method, softened for the mixer method.

Preheat the oven to 350°F /175°C. Spread the pecans in a single layer on a baking sheet and toast for 5 to 7 minutes until fragrant and lightly colored. Cool completely.

Processor Method: Cut the cheddar cheese into ½" to ¾"cubes and set aside. Cut the butter into the same size pieces and keep both cold.

Place the flour, salt, and cayenne pepper in the processor. Pulse several times to mix.

Add the chunks of cheddar cheese and process until the cheese cannot be seen. You will have an orange looking mixture.

Add the cold butter and process until the dough is nearly finished coming together. Do not add water or any liquid to get it to ball up. If necessary, redistribute the dough in the processor to help it along. Process until a ball forms, redistributing as necessary.

When the dough comes together completely, divide into thirds and place them around the processor bowl. Add the pecans. Pulse to cut the nuts into the dough. Do not overprocess or the nuts will become too small. It may be necessary to chill the dough in order to be able to roll it.

Mixer Method: Coarsely chop the nuts. Set aside.

The butter should be softened and the cheese should be grated. Place the butter and cheese in the bowl of a mixer fitted with the paddle attachment. Cream until completely combined.

Add the salt and cayenne pepper, beating to incorporate. Add the flour in 3 parts, mixing each time until completely incorporated. Lastly, add the pecans. It may be necessary to chill the dough in order to be able to roll it.

Shaping

Divide the dough into halves (about 225 grams or 8 ounces each). Roll each into a log 13" to 14" long. Wrap in plastic wrap and refrigerate until firm or up to 3 days.

Preheat the oven to 350°F /175°C. Line baking sheets with parchment paper.

Cut the logs into slices about ¼" thick. Bake for 13 to 15 minutes until lightly colored. Cool completely.

Variations - This snack cookie is easy to change. Here are a couple of examples.

Bleu Cheese Walnut Shortbreads - Substitute Bleu Cheese crumbles for the cheddar cheese. You want to use a firm bleu cheese for these cookies. Substitute toasted walnuts for the pecans.

Caliente Shortbreads - Substitute hot pepper jack or habanero cheese for the cheddar cheese. Add 1 tablespoon powdered cumin and use pumpkin seeds instead of pecans. Chop the pumpkin seeds in the processor first. Remove them and continue as in the original recipe, adding the seeds at the end.

Yield: Approximately 80 shortbreads

Storage: These keep for weeks in an airtight container.

Make Ahead: After the dough is rolled into logs, it can be wrapped in foil and frozen for several months. Defrost in the refrigerator overnight. Slice and bake as above. ◆

Chapter 5
Stuffed and Filled Cookies

IT'S TRUE THAT STUFFED AND filled cookies require a bit more time to make compared to other cookies, but they are a true reward once finished. Stuffed cookies involve shaping cookie dough around a filling, then baking it as one. Filled cookies are simply two cookies sandwiched with a filling in between. There's no going wrong with either one.

Peppermint Ravioli

Caramel-Filled Chocolate Gems

Cookie Pops

Raggedy Ann Cookies

Crème de Menthe Patties

Fig Newtons

Gluten-Free Chocolate Raspberry Cookies

Chocolate Coconut Stuffed Cookies

Mini Chocolate Peanut Butter Whoopie Pies

Ice Cream Sandwiches

Inside Out Oreos

Almost Oreos

Neapolitan Cookies

Peppermint Ravioli

I ALWAYS LOOK FORWARD TO the winter holidays when Ghirardelli sends out their seasonal peppermint squares, just so I can make these Peppermint Ravioli. This once-a-year candy treat is delicious on its own, but reaches a whole new level when incorporated into a cookie. If you're looking for something different to add to that cookie exchange or holiday tray, this could be just the thing. Of course, I can always substitute a different flavor of square during the year.

The dough rolls very easily between two sheets of wax paper, which makes it simple to just pick up, place on a tray, and chill if it softens at any point.

Because of the brief baking time, the peppermint squares don't melt or change shape.

Peppermint Ravioli

3	cups all-purpose flour (420 grams or 14¾ ounces)
¾	cup powdered sugar (100 grams or 3½ ounces)
⅔	teaspoon salt
1½	cups unsalted butter, softened (340 grams, 12 ounces, or 1½ sticks)
2	teaspoons vanilla extract
16	Ghirardelli peppermint squares, either dark or milk chocolate*

*There should be 16 to 18 squares in one bag of Ghirardelli Peppermint Squares.

Preheat the oven to 350°F / 175°C. Line two baking sheets with parchment paper.

Whisk together the flour, sugar, and salt. Set aside.

Beat the butter and vanilla together until creamy. Add the flour mixture all at once and beat just until blended. If the dough is very soft, chill briefly in the refrigerator.

Shaping the Ravioli

Divide the dough into fourths (205 grams or 7⅕ ounce each). Roll one piece between wax paper into a 12½ x 6½ inch rectangle (see wax paper technique on page xlii). I don't know anyone that can do this in one pass. Trim the excess dough and patch around the corners to square them. Roll lightly over the corners to consolidate.

Trim to a 12x6 inch rectangle.

Place 4 equally-spaced peppermint squares on top of the dough and 4 on the bottom, leaving ½" on the ends and 1" between the squares.

Roll a second piece as above. Refrigerate to firm the dough to make it easier to transfer.

Lightly wet the exposed dough around the squares with water.

Remove the top piece of wax paper from the refrig-

erated dough. Pick up from the bottom piece of paper and lower it over the squares. Remove the paper. Let the top dough soften a bit.

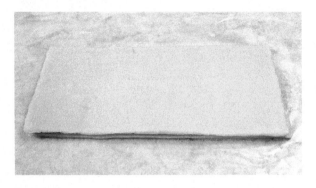

Press the top dough firmly around the squares. If air bubbles form, prick them with a cake tester and press out the air. Make sure the top, bottom, and sides of the cookies are pressed well so the shape of the squares show.

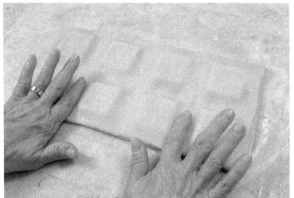

With a fluted pastry cutter or pizza cutter, trim the

outer edges so they are flush.

Cut between the squares and around the edges leaving a ½" overhang. Chill until firm.

Repeat this process with the remaining two pieces of dough.

Place 8 ravioli per baking sheet, staggering them for more room.

Bake at 350°F / 175°C for 10 to 12 minutes until lightly browned. Cool completely. Dust lightly with powdered sugar if desired.

Yield: 16 Peppermint Ravioli

Storage: Store for up to two weeks in an airtight container. ◆

Caramel-Filled Chocolate Gems

THESE ALMOND-COATED AND CARAMEL-FIL-LED CHOCOLATE cookies are ideal anytime, but are especially wonderful on a holiday cookie tray. The cookies are coated in finely chopped almonds. I prefer chopping nuts by hand when they are used to finish or decorate a cookie. Chopping nuts in a food processor is fine if they are being used on the inside of a cookie, but processing produces very uneven cuts and a lot of powder. Regardless of your chopping method, sieve the nuts to remove any powder for the best looking cookie.

The cocoa in this recipe can be natural or Dutch because there is no leavening involved. I use Dutch cocoa because the cookies are darker when baked.

Caramel Filling

see page xxix

½   cup Best Caramel Ever

Make the caramel at least a day before or earlier. It can be covered and stored at room temperature for a couple of days, or refrigerated to keep longer.

Caramel-Filled Chocolate Gems

1   cup slivered almonds (114 grams or 4 ounces)
1   cup all-purpose flour (140 grams or 5 ounces)
⅓   cup cocoa, natural or Dutch (30 grams or 1 ounce)
¼   teaspoon salt
⅔   cup granulated sugar (135 grams or 4¾ ounces)
½   cup unsalted butter, softened (114 grams, 4 ounces, or 1 stick)
1   large egg yolk
2   tablespoons milk
1   teaspoon vanilla extract

Finely chop the almonds and sieve them. Set aside.

Using a strainer, sift the flour, cocoa, and salt together to remove the lumps of cocoa because they won't always break down in mixing. Press any lumps through the strainer with a spoon. Set aside.

Combine the remaining ingredients in the bowl of a mixer. Beat until completely blended. Add the flour mixture and beat until mixed completely. Refrigerate the dough for several hours or up to three days, covered.

When ready to bake, preheat the oven to 350°F / 175°C. Line 2 baking sheets with parchment paper and set aside.

Place the almonds in a small bowl. Using a #100 disher/scooper or a scant tablespoon, drop 2 or 3 balls of dough into the nuts. Scoop up some of the nuts along with a ball of dough. Roll the dough between your hands, pressing the nuts into the ball. Place 4 across and 6 down on the prepared baking sheets.

With the end of a wooden spoon, make a hole almost to the bottom of the cookie (see page xli). Do not go through to the bottom.

Double pan and bake for 11 to 13 minutes until they are puffed slightly but still soft in the centers. During baking, the centers will have risen almost to the top. Immediately upon removing the cookies from the oven, press the centers down again with the wooden spoon to reopen the hole.

Cool completely. These cookies can be made ahead about a week or so, and then filled if desired. When ready to fill, place the cookies on a parchment paper lined baking sheet with a little room between each one. All of the cookies will fit on a half sheet pan.

Assembly
    Cookies
½   cup Best Caramel Ever
1   tablespoon cream
    Spoon with a small tipped spoon (iced tea or baby spoon)

Combine the Best Caramel Ever and cream. Microwave for 15 to 20 seconds until bubbly. Stir to combine.

Immediately after stirring, drop a bit of caramel into the centers of the cookies. Reheat the mixture if the caramel won't drop off the spoon easily.

Set cookies aside until the caramel is firm.

Note: A 4.58 ounce bag of Werther's soft caramels may be substituted. Other caramels may be used, but the amount of cream may have to be adjusted. If using the store-bought caramel, unwrap the caramels and place them in a 1 cup microwave-safe measuring cup or small bowl. Add the cream. Microwave as directed above. This will yield about ½ cup of caramel.

Final Flourish: Melt 1 ounce of semisweet chocolate and drizzle lightly over the cookies.

Yield: About 45 cookies

Storage: After the caramel and/or chocolate has set completely, the cookies can be stored in a closed container with paper between the layers for about a week. ◆

Cookie Pops

WHAT COULD BE MORE FUN than a peanut butter cookie on a stick? How about a peanut butter cookie with a Snickers™ or Simply Caramel™ bar inside! Round wooden sticks can be found in hobby shops. These are preferred over popsicle sticks which are usually flat.

Cookie Pops
13   fun-size Snickers™ or Simply Caramel™ bars
13   wooden sticks, preferably round
1½   cup all-purpose flour (210 grams or 7⅓ ounces)

½	teaspoon baking powder
½	teaspoon baking soda
¼	teaspoon salt
½	cup unsalted butter, softened (4 ounces, 114 grams, or 1 stick)
½	cup granulated sugar (100 grams or 3½ ounces)
½	cup packed light or dark brown sugar (100 grams or 3½ ounces)
½	cup creamy peanut butter* (125 grams or 4⅓ ounces)
1	large egg
1	teaspoon vanilla extract

*Use Jif or Peter Pan or another equivalent for this recipe. Natural peanut butter is not recommended.

Prepare the candy bars by inserting a stick into each center about halfway through. Put them in the freezer to harden.

Preheat the oven to 350°F / 175°C. Line several baking sheets with parchment paper. Set aside.

Mix the flour, baking powder, baking soda, and salt in a bowl. Set aside.

Cream the butter and both sugars until light and fluffy. Add the peanut butter and mix to combine well. Add the egg and vanilla. Finally, add the flour mixture and mix until fully incorporated and the dough cleans the sides of the bowl.

Using a #16 disher/scooper or a scant ⅓ cup, scoop 13 balls of dough.

Flatten the balls between your hands.

Center the candy bar on the dough.

Pulling the dough in on both sides, completely wrap the candy bar in the peanut butter cookie.

Seal the edges and top. Be sure that the bottom is well-sealed by pinching it around the stick. Roll between your hands so it looks like a corn dog.

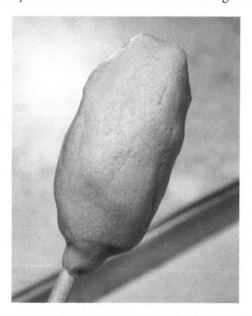

Place the cookie pop on the prepared baking sheet with the seam side down. Continue this process until they are all wrapped. Work as quickly as you can so the candy remains frozen when it goes into the oven. On the baking sheet, place 2 at the top, 2 at the bottom, and 1 in the middle.

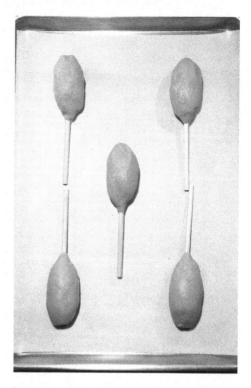

Bake for 12 to 15 minutes until golden brown. Cool completely.

Yield: 13 cookie pops

Storage: Store in a closed container at room temperature for 3 to 4 days. These freeze well before or after baking. If baked, thaw at room temperature. If frozen, preheat the oven to 350°F / 175°C. Thaw the cookie pops for 20 minutes at room temperature, then bake as above. ◆

Raggedy Ann Cookies

THIS BEGAN AS ONE COOKIE then became another as I saw its endless possibilities. There are times when I am just not in the mood to roll and cut out cookies. Cut-out cookies are precise and beautiful, and these Raggedy Ann Cookies are not; but they are very versatile, easy, and quicker to make. The name comes from the homey look of these cookies with their sometimes raggedy edges. I've included three fillings, but anything goes with these delights.

Freeze-dried raspberries make an intensely sharp raspberry filling. No one will be able to figure out how you got so much raspberry flavor into the buttercream unless you tell them (or they have the book)! Homemade caramel and chocolate round out the three fillings.

Raggedy Ann Cookies

¾   cup walnuts (3 ounces or 85 grams)
2   cups all-purpose flour (280 grams or 10 ounces)
¼   teaspoon salt
1   cup unsalted butter, softened (225 grams, 8 ounces, or 2 sticks)
¾   cup granulated sugar (150 grams or 5¼ ounces)
1   large egg
1   teaspoon vanilla extract
    Granulated sugar as needed
    Filling of choice (below)

Preheat the oven to 350°F / 175°C. Spread the walnuts in a single layer on a rimmed baking sheet. Toast to a medium brown for about 7 to 9 minutes, depending on the size of the walnuts. Cool completely. Lower the heat of the oven to 325°F / 163°C. Line baking sheets with parchment paper and set aside.

When the nuts have cooled, process them with about ½ cup (70 grams or 2½ ounces) of the measured flour. They should be finely ground. Mix with the remaining flour and salt, and set aside.

Combine the butter and sugar in the bowl of a mixer and beat until very light and fluffy. Add the egg and vanilla. Beat until incorporated, scraping the sides of the bowl as needed.

Add the flour mixture all at once, beating on low speed until it comes together.

Refrigerate the dough for about an hour to firm. Using a #100 disher/scooper or about 2 teaspoons of dough per cookie, drop balls of dough onto the prepared baking sheets. The dough will soften quickly so chill as needed. Roll the scoops into balls and chill.

Place the balls 4 across and 6 down on the baking sheet. With the bottom of a glass dipped in granulated sugar, press the ball down to form a 2" round.

Bake the cookies for 6 minutes, then turn the pan and bake about 6 to 7 minutes more or until set.

Cool. Sandwich generously with one of the fillings below, or use a combination.

Raspberry Buttercream

1½   ounces freeze-dried raspberries (45 grams)
1¾   cups powdered sugar (200 grams or 7 ounces)
½   cup unsalted butter, softened (114 grams, 4 ounces, or 1 stick)
3   to 4 tablespoons milk
     Red food coloring

Remove the package of drying agent from the freeze-dried raspberries. Be sure to have the processor stopper in place, or some of the raspberry powder will escape while processing. Place the raspberries and about half of the powdered sugar in the processor bowl, and process until the raspberries are powdered. Scrape the sides of the bowl often.

Combine the raspberry mixture, remaining powdered sugar, butter, and milk in the bowl of a mixer. Beat on low speed to combine. Raise the speed to medium, and then to high to lighten the mixture and build volume. Scrape the sides and bottom of the bowl several times.

Add red food coloring to obtain a pleasing color. Sandwich the cookies with the buttercream or the fillings below.

Caramel Filling

1   recipe Best Caramel Ever, page xxix.

Heat or microwave the caramel briefly to make it spreadable.

Chocolate Filling

6   ounces semisweet chocolate (170 grams)
2   tablespoons shortening

Melt chocolate and shortening together over a double boiler or in the microwave at half power. Whisk to combine. Cool or chill briefly to set it up.

Yield: About 36 sandwiched cookies

Storage: Keep for 10 days or more in an airtight container. ◆

Créme De Menthe Patties

THIS IS ONE OF THE most exciting cookies in this book. A chocolate peppermint cookie is covered with a butter mint patty, then enrobed in a chocolate coating that dries to a semi-gloss finish. Unlike ganache, when this coating is completely set, it can be picked up without getting chocolate all over your hands.

Either natural or Dutch cocoa can be used. I use Dutch cocoa as it makes a darker cookie.

Chocolate Cookies

½   cup powdered sugar (65 grams or 2¼ ounces)

¼   cup cocoa, natural or Dutch (25 grams or .87 ounce)

½   cup unsalted butter, softened (114 grams, 4 ounces, or 1 stick)

½   teaspoon peppermint extract

1   cup cake flour (125 grams or about 4⅓ ounces)

Preheat the oven to 350°F / 175°C. Line baking sheets with parchment paper and set aside.

Sift the powdered sugar and cocoa together. Combine this mixture in a mixing bowl with the butter and peppermint extract. Beat until light. It will look like fudge. Add the flour and beat on low speed until completely mixed.

If the dough is too soft to roll into a log, refrigerate briefly until firm enough. Otherwise, divide the dough in half and roll it into a 15" log.

When ready to bake, let the logs rest at room temperature. They should be firm, but not hard. Cut into slices ⅓" thick and place on the prepared baking sheets.

Double pan and bake for 18 to 20 minutes until they are just set. Cool.

Crème de Menthe Patties

1   tablespoon unsalted butter, melted

1   tablespoon milk

½   teaspoon peppermint extract

1½   cup powdered sugar (200 grams or 7 ounces)

Line a baking sheet with parchment paper.

Combine the melted butter, milk, and peppermint extract. Add it to the powdered sugar. Stir until it somewhat comes together. Turn out onto a work area and knead until smooth but still pliable. It will resemble fondant. If it is too dry, add milk a tiny bit at a time. Shape into a smooth ball.

Roll between wax paper to about ⅛" thickness (see wax paper technique on page xlii). Cut out rounds using a 1½" plain cutter. Place on the prepared baking sheet. Keep the rounds covered with plastic wrap as you cut them so they don't dry out. Reroll the scraps to make enough rounds to cover all the cookies.

Place one round on top of each chocolate cookie. If they don't fit exactly to the edge of the cookies, nudge the patty into the shape of the cookie by pushing out from the center of the patty to the edge. Keep these covered with plastic wrap until you finish.

Chocolate Coating

The coating should be able to be poured over the cookies and completely enrobe them. Try coating one cookie, then adjust the consistency if necessary.

1½   cups powdered sugar (200 grams or 7 ounces)
6   tablespoons cocoa, natural or Dutch (35 grams or 1¼ ounces)
1   tablespoon light corn syrup
¼   cup water

Sift the powdered sugar and cocoa together. Stir to mix completely.

Combine the corn syrup and water. Add to the sugar/cocoa mixture and stir to combine. If too dense, adjust the consistency by adding more water a tiny bit at a time. If too runny, add more powdered sugar.

Place a cooling rack over wax paper or foil and place a few cookies on the rack. Use a serving spoon to pour the coating over each cookie. Inspect the cookie to make sure it has been fully covered. If not, you can dab a bit of coating on any spots left uncovered.

Let them dry for a while on the rack, then transfer them to a foil-lined surface to dry completely.

Yield: About 35 cookies

Storage: Store in a container with wax paper between the layers for several days.

Make Ahead: The unbaked logs can be frozen, wrapped in foil, and kept in the freezer for several months. Thaw in the refrigerator, then bake and finish as above. ◆

Fig Newtons

THIS IS A NOT-TOO-SWEET RENDITION of Fig Newtons™ that look exactly like their namesake. They are not a difficult cookie to make, and are perfect with tea or coffee. In fact, I eat them for breakfast, with my tea, if they happen to be laying around!

I use dried, but moist, black mission figs so they don't need to be soaked. I have given instructions for softening drier figs, but the amount of water they will require in this recipe (if any) may vary.

It is best to make these cookies at least a day before serving, as their flavor will be enhanced and they will soften slightly.

Dough for the Fig Newtons

2⅓   cups all-purpose flour (325 grams or about 11½ ounces)
2   teaspoons baking powder
½   teaspoon baking soda
½   teaspoon salt
6   tablespoons unsalted butter, softened (90 grams or 3 ounces)

⅔ cup packed light brown sugar (130 grams 4½ ounces)

2 large eggs

1 teaspoon vanilla extract

Whisk together the flour, baking powder, baking soda, and salt. Set aside.

Beat the butter and sugar until light and fluffy. Add the eggs and vanilla, and mix on medium to medium-high speed until combined. Scrape down the sides of the bowl often. Don't worry if the mixture curdles after a couple of minutes.

Add the flour mixture all at once and beat until the dough comes together. Remove from the bowl and divide into thirds (about 175 grams or 6 ounces each). Shape into 4x6 inch rectangles, wrap in plastic wrap, and refrigerate at least 2 hours or overnight.

Filling

Make this just before using

2½ cups moist black mission figs* (400 grams)

½ cup granulated sugar (100 grams or 3½ ounces)

2 teaspoons vanilla extract

2 to 3 tablespoons water

*If using really dry figs, place them in a saucepan covered with water and bring to a boil. Reduce the heat to a simmer and cook until soft, but not squishy. Remove them from the water and let cool. Squeeze out any excess water and proceed as instructed below, omitting the water. If the mixture is not spreadable, add water sparingly until the right consistency is reached.

Otherwise, combine the figs, sugar, and vanilla in the bowl of a processor. Process until they form a rough paste. Add 2 tablespoons water and process to make a spreadable paste. If the mixture is still too stiff, add additional water a tiny bit at a time. The filling should be easily spreadable but not runny.

Divide into thirds (about 175 grams or 6 ounces each).

Assembly

Preheat the oven to 350°F / 175°C. Line a baking sheet with parchment paper and set aside.

Refrigerate two pieces of dough, and roll the third into a 5½ x13 inch rectangle between wax paper (see wax paper technique on page xlii).

Mark the dough 1¾" in from both sides through the wax paper. Leaving the wax paper in place, chill the dough while rolling the other two pieces.

To fill, remove the top piece of wax paper on one of the rectangles leaving the dough on the bottom piece. Spread one third of the filling down the center.

At this point, the dough should be soft enough to fold over. If not, let it sit for a few minutes. Using the wax paper to assist, fold one side of the dough over the filling.

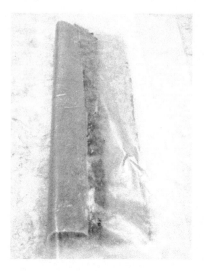

Wet the edge of the opposite side of the dough, and again using the wax paper, lift to cover the filling about ½" over the center edge of dough. Gently press the seam down so it adheres to the bottom piece of dough.

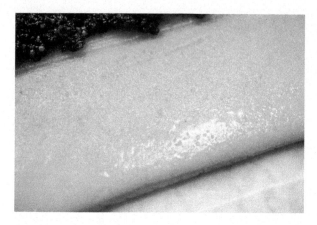

Leaving the roll on the wax paper, transfer it to a baking sheet. Refrigerate while preparing the other two pieces of dough and fillings in the same manner.

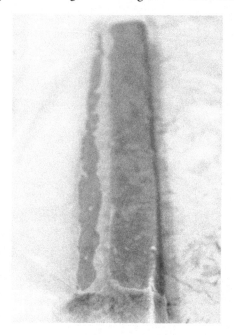

Refrigerate the rolls until firm enough to easily remove them from the wax paper.

When firm, remove the rolls from the wax paper.

Place them, seam side down, on the parchment paper lined baking sheet about 2" apart.

Bake for 18 to 20 minutes until golden brown. Cool briefly.

While still warm, using a serrated knife and a sawing motion, cut each roll into 1" slices. Rinse and dry the knife every few cuts for the prettiest cookies.

The cookies will be firm when just baked but will soften when stored.

Yield: About 36 to 40 cookies

Storage: Store in an airtight container for a week or more. ◆

Gluten-Free Chocolate Raspberry Cookies

THE ORIGINAL RECIPE FOR THESE super chewy and rich flourless chocolate cookies comes from King Arthur Flour, but of course, I had to put in my 2 cents. This gluten-free and almost fat-free cookie comes together quickly with just a whisk and a bowl, or a hand mixer, and bakes in minutes. While they are good by themselves, they are even better sandwiched together with raspberry jam and sprinkled with powdered sugar. These Gluten-Free Chocolate Raspberry Cookies are amazingly fudgy and moist and have quickly become a favorite even for those that can have gluten.

Gluten-Free Chocolate Raspberry Cookies

2¼	cups powdered sugar (255 grams or 9 ounces)
¼	teaspoon salt
1	cup cocoa, preferably Dutch (85 grams or 3 ounces)

2   teaspoons vanilla extract

1   teaspoon instant coffee or espresso powder

3   large egg whites (100 grams or 3½ ounces)
     Raspberry jam as needed, preferably seedless

Preheat the oven to 350°F /175°C. Line 3 baking sheets with parchment paper and spray with non-stick baking release. This is an important step because the cookies won't spread as they should without it.

Sift the powdered sugar, salt, and cocoa together in a bowl to remove any lumps. Set aside.

Stir together the vanilla and coffee. Add to the egg whites, and pour the mixture over the dry ingredients. Whisk together or use a mixer on low speed to combine completely. The batter will be very thick and shiny.

Using a #100 disher/scooper or a level half tablespoon, drop the dough onto the prepared baking sheets. Drop 15 cookies, three across and five down, as they need plenty of room to spread. Repeat with remaining dough.

Bake for 7 minutes. Do not overbake or they will be dry.

The cookies will be a little shiny, somewhat puffy, and have faintly crackled tops. Cool completely on the parchment paper before removing them. They should just peel off the parchment paper, but if not, use a pancake turner to loosen them.

Pair the cookies by matching size and shape, and sandwich them together with a bit of raspberry jam. Sprinkle lightly with powdered sugar.

Yield: About 45 2¼" cookies or 22 sandwiched cookies. For smaller cookies, drop by half an iced tea spoon, 4 across and 6 down. Bake 6 minutes. This will make about 72 cookies or 36 sandwiched cookies.

Storage: These store well in a closed container for several days. ◆

Chocolate Coconut Stuffed Cookies

A PHOTOGRAPH OF THIS COOKIE has been in my files for over 25 years. It was from an ad for a cookie sold to retail establishments. For some reason, I never did anything with it. I just looked at it. When I was gathering information for this book, I moved it over to my current file and here it is!

If you love coconut or Mounds bars, this is your cookie. A deep chocolate brownie cookie enfolds a coconut macaroon. One thing that makes these so appealing is the use of both sweetened and unsweetened coconut.

The combination of sweetened coconut and sweetened condensed milk is often too sweet. The use of unsweetened coconut solves this problem. You will notice that both have the same weight, but are vastly different in volume. That is because the sweetened coconut is very moist, making it heavier. The unsweetened coconut is very dry, almost fluffy. Unsweetened coconut is also known as desiccated coconut.

Coconut Macaroons

¾ cup sweetened condensed milk

¾ cup sweetened coconut (70 grams or approximately 2½ ounces)

1½ cup unsweetened coconut (70 grams or approximately 2½ ounces)

1 teaspoon vanilla extract

Line a baking sheet with parchment paper.

Combine all of the ingredients in the bowl of a mixer. Using a packed #60 disher/scooper or a packed tablespoon, drop mounds of the mixture onto the prepared baking sheet. As the mixture will be very sticky, freeze the mounds to make them easier to roll into balls. When partially or even completely frozen, roll the mounds into balls. Place them back into the freezer.

Wet your hands a little to make the rolling easier.

Yield: 16 balls

Chocolate Brownie Cookies

1⅓ cups all-purpose flour (185 grams or 6½ ounces)

½ teaspoon baking powder

½ teaspoon salt

½ cup Dutch cocoa (45 grams or 1½ ounces)

1 cup granulated sugar (200 grams or 7 ounces)

½ cup unsalted butter, melted (114 grams, 4 ounces, or 1 stick)

2 tablespoons vegetable oil

1 large egg

2 teaspoons vanilla extract

Preheat the oven to 350°F / 175°C. Line 2 baking sheets with parchment paper and set aside.

Whisk the flour, baking powder, and salt together. Set aside.

In the bowl of a mixer, combine the cocoa, sugar, butter, vegetable oil, egg, and vanilla. Beat to blend completely. Add the flour mixture all at once beating on low speed until the dough comes together smoothly.

Drop two scoops of dough on top of each other using a #60 disher/scooper. Alternatively, use two tablespoons per cookie. Combine the scoops by rolling each into a ball, and place on a prepared baking sheet. There will be 16 to 17 balls.

On the parchment paper, flatten one ball of dough to about a 3" round. Place a frozen coconut ball in the middle.

Pull the sides up around the coconut ball and

push the dough to the middle to completely enclose the filling. Roll between your hands and place seam side down on the parchment paper.

Place 8 balls on a half sheet pan. **Double pan** and bake for 12 to 13 minutes. They will be soft coming from the oven but will firm up slightly upon cooling.

Cool completely.

Yield: 16 cookies

Storage: These will keep well for 5 to 6 days stored in an airtight container. They may also be frozen, completely baked, for several months. Simply thaw on a rack at room temperature.

Chocolate Brownie Cookies *Variation:* I had enough brownie dough to make one brownie cookie using 2 tablespoons of dough. Omit the coconut filling. Add ⅔ cup chocolate chips or walnuts, or half of each to the dough. Drop by 2 scoops using #60 disher/scooper, or 2 tablespoons per cookie. This makes about about 20 cookies. **Double pan** and bake as above for 12 minutes. ◆

Mini Chocolate Peanut Butter Whoopie Pies

I LOVE MINI ANYTHING, AND these are a perfect two-bite treat. The combination of chocolate and peanut butter is a favorite all-American flavor. The real secret to whoopie pies is to overfill them. A skimpy filling is the worst thing you can do to this cookie.

While the classic whoopie pie has a marshmallow cream-based filling, I found this filling more suitable for these very moist chocolate cookies. In fact, they are not cookies, they are actually mini cakes.

Chocolate Mini Cakes

2 cups all-purpose flour (280 grams or 10 ounces)

½ cup Dutch cocoa (45 grams or 1½ ounces)

1¼ teaspoon baking soda

¾ teaspoon salt

½ cup unsalted butter, softened (114 grams, 4 ounces, or 1 stick)

1 cup packed light or dark brown sugar (200 grams or 7 ounces)

1 teaspoon vanilla extract

1 large egg

1 cup buttermilk

Preheat the oven to 350°F / 175°C. Line 3 baking sheets with parchment paper and set aside.

Sift together the flour, cocoa, baking soda, and salt. Set aside.

In the bowl of a mixer, beat the butter, sugar, and vanilla until light and fluffy. Add the egg. The mixture may appear curdled but that is fine.

Alternate adding the flour mixture and buttermilk, starting and ending with the flour. I usually add the flour 4 times and the buttermilk 3 times.

Using a number #70 disher/scooper or a rounded tablespoon, scoop the batter and place 4 across and 6 down on the prepared baking sheets. There will be a total of 24 mounds on each baking sheet, spaced well apart. They don't have to be perfect as they will round out in the oven, but keep in rounded mounds as much as possible.

There will be about 72 cookies.

Bake 8 to 9 minutes until just set and the cakes spring back when lightly touched. Let them cool on the baking sheet.

Peanut Butter Filling

¾ cup creamy peanut butter (170 grams or 6 ounces)*

4 tablespoons unsalted butter, softened (60 grams, 2 ounces, or ½ stick)

1¾ cup powdered sugar (225 grams or 8 ounces)

1 teaspoon vanilla extract

2 to 3 tablespoons milk

*Jif, Peter Pan, or another commercial peanut butter is best for this recipe. Natural peanut butter will alter the outcome.

Combine the peanut butter, butter, powdered sugar, vanilla, and 2 tablespoons milk in the bowl of a mixer. Beat until light, smooth, and airy. Add more milk, a bit at a time, if the filling is too tight.

Match the cookies by size and shape, and turn half of them upside-down. Generously pipe or spoon on the filling. If piping, a ⅜" plain or star tip works perfectly. Top with a second cookie.

Yield: 36 sandwiched cookies

Storage: Keep in a container for a few days or freeze to keep longer.

Note: These can be made larger if desired. Just use a larger disher/scooper or spoon. Bake 2 to 3 minutes longer but do not overbake. ◆

Ice Cream Sandwiches

THESE TERRIFIC ICE CREAM SANDWICHES feature an easily made no-churn strawberry ice cream sandwiched between two chocolate cookies. These will please all ice cream lovers… both young and old! The cookies are great all by themselves, or paired with lightly sweetened fresh fruit. The sandwiches can be shaped into squares or rounds as you please.

The ice cream, which uses two types of strawberries to intensify the flavor, is easy to make as it doesn't require an ice cream machine. It goes together in minutes while it awaits the chocolate cookies.

No-Churn Strawberry Ice Cream
1   2 ounce package freeze-dried strawberries (34 grams)*
1   cup fresh strawberries, coarsely chopped
1¼ cups heavy cream
⅔   cup condensed milk

*This size package can be found at Trader's Joes.

Line a 9x9x2 inch pan with foil overhanging two sides for handles. Set aside.

Remove the desiccant package from the freeze-dried strawberries. Process the strawberries until they are powdery with some very small pieces remaining. Remove from the processor.

Finely chop the fresh strawberries by hand, or pulse in the processor to make 1 cup.

Whip the cream to medium stiff peaks.

Mix the condensed milk and both strawberry types together. Fold this mixture into the cream. Pour into the prepared pan and freeze.

When frozen, cut 3 across and 3 down for nine 3" squares of ice cream. Alternatively, cut out 3" rounds with a cookie cutter. Place back in the freezer. The ice cream will keep for weeks well-wrapped in the pan.

Chocolate Cookies

2½ cups all-purpose flour (350 grams or 12¼ ounces)

½ cup cocoa, natural or Dutch* (45 grams or about 1½ ounces)

¾ cup powdered sugar (90 grams or 3 ounces)

¾ teaspoon salt

1½ cups unsalted butter, softened (285 grams, 10 ounces, or 2½ sticks)

2 teaspoons vanilla extract

*Dutch cocoa makes a darker cookie, but natural cocoa can also be used.

Preheat oven to 350°F / 175°C. Line baking sheets with parchment paper and set aside.

Sift together the flour, cocoa, sugar, and salt. Set aside.

Beat the butter and vanilla until creamy. Add the flour mixture until just blended. Chill the dough if it is too soft to roll. Otherwise, roll half the dough (390 grams or 12⅔ ounces each) into a 10x10 inch rectangle about ¼" thick between wax paper (see wax paper technique on page xlii). Trim the edges to make a 9x9 inch square. Mark 3 across and 3 down for 9 squares and cut, but do not separate.

If making round sandwiches, cut the dough into 9 3" rounds with a cookie cutter.

Prick each cookie with a fork 4 or 5 times. Freeze until hard.

Remove from the freezer and break the squares apart. Place on the prepared baking sheets.

Repeat with the second half of dough. There will be 18 chocolate cookies.

Double pan and bake 14 to 16 minutes until very firm. If they lump up in the middle after baking, gently flatten them with a pancake turner immediately upon removing from the oven.

Cool completely. The cookies will store for days in a covered container.

Assembly

3" Chocolate Cookies
    Strawberry Ice Cream

Sandwich one square or round of ice cream between 2 cookies. Keep in the freezer until serving. If storing more than a day or two, wrap each individually in foil.

Yield: 9 ice cream sandwiches

Storage: Wrapped in foil, these will store for up to a month in the freezer. ◆

Inside Out Oreos

THESE COOKIES USE AN UNUSUAL leavening agent – baker's ammonia, also called ammonium carbonate. It is used quite often in European cookies. This ingredient yields a very crisp and airy cookie that doesn't lose its crispness when stored. It smells very strong in the bottle, but no hint can be found in the baked cookies. Fair warning, don't take a whiff. It is the same stuff they use to bring people to if they have fainted – it packs a punch!

Baking powder is listed as an alternative, but it will not make the same crisp cookie.

These cookies are as addictive as their counterpart. The textural difference between the crispy cookie and the fudgy filling is particularly amazing.

Inside Out Oreos

1 tablespoon vanilla extract
½ teaspoon ammonium carbonate **OR** 1½
   teaspoon baking powder
1 cup unsalted butter, softened (225 grams, 8 ounces, or 2 sticks)
1¼ cups granulated sugar (250 grams or 8¾ ounces)
1¾ cups all-purpose flour (245 grams or about 8⅔ ounces)
¾ teaspoon salt
   Granulated sugar as needed

Preheat the oven to 350°F / 175°C. Line several baking sheets with parchment paper. Set aside.

If using ammonium carbonate: Combine the vanilla and ammonium carbonate in a small bowl. Stir to dissolve the ammonia.

Add the vanilla mixture, butter, and sugar to the bowl of a mixer. Beat until smooth. Add the flour and salt, beating until the dough comes together.

If using baking powder: Combine the flour, salt, and baking powder. Set aside. Add vanilla, butter, and sugar to the bowl of a mixer. Beat until smooth. Add the flour mixure beating until the dough comes together.

For both versions: The dough may initially seem too dry, but it will come together. Scrape down the sides of the bowl often, and redistribute the mixture to help it along.

With a #100 disher/scooper, or 2 teaspoons of dough per cookie, drop about 1½" apart on the prepared baking sheets. Roll between your hands to form smooth balls.

Dip the bottom of a glass into granulated sugar, and flatten the balls into ¼" thick rounds.

Bake the cookies for about 15 minutes until they

are lightly browned. If you used the ammonia, you will smell it at this point. Don't worry, that is as it should be! It is harmless and will dissipate.

Cool the cookies completely.

Chocolate Filling

½ cup heavy cream
¼ cup corn syrup (70 grams or 2½ ounces)
10 ounces semisweet chocolate (285 grams)
2¼ cups powdered sugar, sifted (300 grams or 10½ ounces)

In a small saucepan, heat the cream and corn syrup just to a simmer. Submerge the chocolate under the hot mixture. Wait a few minutes, then whisk gently to bring it together. Cool completely.

In the meantime, sift the measured powdered sugar. Place the chocolate mixture and powdered sugar in the bowl of a mixer. Beat just to combine, but no more.

Pair cookies by size and shape. With a #60 disher/scooper or a tablespoon measure, drop filling into the center of the underside of one of the cookies. Top with a second cookie, right side up, and press together lightly to bring the filling to the edge. Allow the filling to set up in the cookies.

Yield: About 60 single cookies or 30 sandwiched cookies

Storage: Once the filling has completely set, the cookies can be stored in an airtight container for a week to 10 days. ◆

Almost Oreos

I HAVE KNOWN ABOUT BLACK Cocoa for a while, but my interest was piqued when I saw a recipe on King Arthur's blog using it for "Faux-Reos." The cookies were indeed as black as a moonless night far away from the city lights. To say I was intrigued was an understatement.

I found Black Onyx cocoa powder online. It is Dutch cocoa that has been alkalized to the extreme. When raw, it has a purplish color. The cookies, without the filling, are almost as compelling due to their crispiness and flavor. In fact, I thought they tasted just like the Oreo™ chocolate cookie. I originally posted this recipe on my blog for Halloween, hence the colored fillings.

King Arthur came up with a great way to emboss these cookies, using the end of the plunger for a food processor. If you don't have one available, the cookies are just as good without it.

Almost Oreos Chocolate Cookies

1¼ cup all-purpose flour (175 grams or about 6 ounces)

¾ cup Black cocoa* (64 grams or 2¼ ounces)

½ teaspoon salt

¾ cup unsalted butter, softened (170 grams, 6 ounces, or 1½ sticks)

1 cup + 2 tablespoons granulated sugar (225 grams or 8 ounces)

1 large egg

1 teaspoon vanilla extract

Granulated sugar as needed

*Regular Dutch cocoa can be used if necessary, but the color will not be as dark and they may not be as crisp.

Preheat the oven to 325°F / 163°C. Line several baking sheets with parchment paper and set aside.

Sift the flour, cocoa, and salt together. Set aside.

Beat the butter and sugar together. Add the egg and vanilla, and beat to combine. If it curdles, increase the speed of the mixer and continue beating. Don't worry if it remains curdled.

Add the flour mixture and beat to combine, scraping down the sides of the bowl several times.

Refrigerate the dough for about 1½ hours or up to several days.

Using a #60 disher/scooper or a tablespoon of dough per cookie, scoop the dough about 3 cookies at a time. Roll between your hands into balls and place them, 3 across and 5 down on the prepared baking sheets.

Do not shape too many balls at once or they will soften to the point of not being able to be embossed. If embossing them, dip the end of a food processor plunger into granulated sugar and flatten the balls to about ⅛" thickness. The first couple of cookies may stick to the plunger. Just carefully peel them away. As the plunger gets sticky, the sugar will adhere to it and not to the cookie; simply wipe, redip, and continue embossing. If you are not embossing them, flatten them with the bottom of a glass, dipping it in sugar as above.

If the balls are too cold they will splay at the edges. Let them sit for a minute or so and they will be fine. It doesn't matter if they splay because they will taste just as good.

Place the cookies 3 across and 5 down on the baking sheets.

Double pan and bake for 20 to 22 minutes until completely set with no soft spots. It is very important to double pan or the cookies will burn.

Yield: About 60 single cookies

Filling

2½ cups powdered sugar (285 grams or 10 ounces)
½   cup unsalted butter, softened (114 grams, 4 ounces, or 1 stick)
1   teaspoon vanilla extract
     Food coloring (if tinting the fillings)

Place the sugar, butter, and vanilla in the bowl of a mixer and beat until combined. Continue beating to increase the volume and make it fluffy. If tinting, add food coloring at the end.

Match cookies by size and shape and turn 30 upside-down. (Here's a hint: Put your less attractive cookies on the bottom.) Using a #60 disher/scooper or 1 tablespoon measure, drop a ball of buttercream in the middle of these 30 cookies.

Place another cookie, right side up, on top of the buttercream and gently press down to bring the buttercream to the edge of the cookie.

Let them sit at room temperature so the buttercream can set up.

Yield: 30 sandwiched cookies

Storage: These can be stored in an airtight container for a while. After all, they're Almost Oreos™! ◆

Neapolitan Cookies

THIS COOKIE IS ALMOST HABIT forming. The base cookie is the same cookie used in the Crème de Menthe Patties and the top cookie is almond. Between them is an intense strawberry buttercream made with freeze-dried strawberries.

This cookie dough is easily made and rolled into logs. Following a short chill in the refrigerator, they are quickly sliced into rounds. For some reason, the chocolate cookie bakes up smaller than the almond one, so I compensated for this in the shaping of the chocolate rolls.

These Neapolitan cookies are easy, good-looking, and unique. There isn't much more you can expect from a cookie!

Chocolate Cookies

½   cup powdered sugar (65 grams or 2¼ ounces)
¼   cup cocoa, natural or Dutch (25 grams or .87 ounce)*
½   cup unsalted butter, softened (114 grams, 4 ounces, or 1 stick)
1   teaspoon vanilla extract
1   cup cake flour (125 grams or about 4⅓ ounces)

*Dutch cocoa will make a darker cookie, but natural can be used.

Sift the powdered sugar and cocoa together in a mixing bowl. Add the butter and vanilla, and beat until light. It will look like fudge.

Add the flour and beat on low speed until completely incorporated.

If the dough is too soft to roll into a log, refrigerate it briefly until firm enough. Otherwise, roll into a 14" log. Refrigerate until firm to make it easier to cut. The rolls can be kept well-wrapped in the refrigerator for up to 3 days.

Preheat the oven to 350°F / 175°C. Line several baking sheets with parchment paper and set aside.

When ready to bake, let the logs sit at room temperature for a few minutes. They should be firm, but not hard. Cut into ¼" slices and place on the prepared baking sheets.

Double pan and bake for 18 to 20 minutes until they are just set. Cool.

Yield: About 50 cookies

Almond Cookies

½   cup powdered sugar (65 grams or 2¼ ounces)
½   cup unsalted butter, softened (114 grams, 4 ounces, or 1 stick)
2   teaspoons almond extract
1 cup + 2 tablespoons cake flour (150 grams or about 5¼ ounces)

Combine the powdered sugar, butter, and almond extract in the bowl of a mixer. Beat until light.

Add the flour and beat on low until completely mixed.

Shape into a 15" log and continue as above.

Double pan and bake for 12 to 14 minutes until lightly browned and set. Cool.

Yield: About 50 cookies

Strawberry Buttercream

1.5   ounce package freeze-dried strawberries (45 grams)
1¾   cup powdered sugar (200 grams or 7 ounces)
½   cup unsalted butter, softened (114 grams, 4 ounces, or 1 stick)
½   teaspoon almond extract
3   to 4 tablespoons milk
      Red food coloring
2   ounces semisweet chocolate (60 grams)

Before processing the strawberries, be sure to remove the little package of drying agent in the bag. I mention this because I have forgotten twice, and I had to throw away the whole batch of strawberries and powdered sugar!

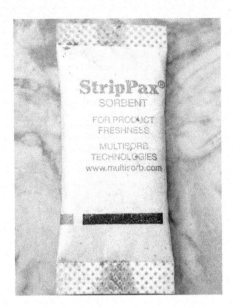

After removing the drying agent, place the strawberries and powdered sugar in the bowl of a processor or blender. Pulverize the strawberries until the powdered sugar turns pink and no strawberries are visible.

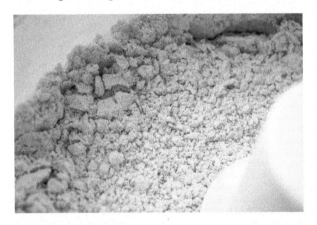

Place the strawberry mixture, butter, and almond extract in a mixing bowl. Add 3 tablespoons of milk and mix on low speed until blended. Increase to medium-high speed and beat for several minutes to lighten the buttercream and increase the volume. Scrape the sides of the bowl often. Add additional milk a little bit at a time if needed to facilitate mixing.

Add red food coloring as needed to reach a pleasing color.

Assembly

Match cookies by size and shape. With a ¼" plain pastry tip, pipe the buttercream on the underside of a chocolate cookie leaving about ⅛" around the rim. Alternatively, use a spoon to scoop, spread, and smooth the buttercream on the cookie.

Top with an almond cookie and press down gently to bring the buttercream to the edges.

Melt the chocolate at half power in the microwave. Dip a spoon in the melted chocolate and wave it airily over the cookies. Let the chocolate set. To hurry the process, chill in the refrigerator or freezer for a few minutes.

It is important to fill the cookies several hours before serving because the strawberry buttercream needs time to fully develop its flavor. It is beyond wonderful when it does!

Yield: About 50 sandwiched cookies

Storage: When the buttercream and chocolate drizzle are firm, store in an airtight container for 7 to 10 days. The cookies may be frozen for several months. Thaw on cooling racks. ◆

Chapter 6
Bar Cookies

BAR COOKIES MAKE THE MOST amount of cookies for the least amount of work. There is no dropping, shaping, rolling or stuffing. Just mix the ingredients, spread them in a pan, bake, cool, and cut. It doesn't get much easier.

Caramel Crunch Toffee Bars

No-Bake Peanut Butter Bars

Banana Split Bars

Cheesecake Bars

Pecan Bars

Chocolate Raspberry Squares

Dutch Apple Crumb Bars

Hawaiian Carrot Cake Squares

Hermit Bars

Almond Raspberry Triangles

Lemon Bars Updated

Chocolate Cheesecake Bars

Evelyn's Chewy Peanut Butter Bars

Lemon-Steeped Gingerbread Squares

Pecan Pie Squares

(Almost) S'Mores Bars

Triple-Layer Pecan Bars

Hazelnut Crunch Bars

Creamy Lime Bars

Rugelach Bars

Caramel Crunch
Toffee Bars

PERHAPS ONE OF THE FAVORITES at the bakery (at least mine), these are also referred to as Millionaire's shortbread as well as many other names. A crisp, buttery shortbread base is topped with a deep, smooth, rich caramel, and finished with chocolate and crunchy toffee bits. We always looked forward to making these so we could eat the trims!

Caramel
1   Recipe Best Caramel Ever, cooked to 242°F / 117°C, see page xxix

Shortbread Base
1½   cups all-purpose flour (210 grams flour 7⅓ ounces)

½   cup powdered sugar (65 grams or 2¼ ounces)

¾   cup + 1 tablespoon unsalted butter, cold and cut into small pieces (195 grams, about 6¾ ounces, or 1½ sticks + 1 tablespoon)

Preheat the oven to 350°F / 175°C. Line the bottom of a 9x9x2 inch pan with parchment paper. Spray the paper and sides of the pan with a non-stick baking release.

Place the flour and powdered sugar in the bowl of a processor. Process to mix. Add the cold butter and process until indistinguishable. See Press in Crusts page xxxviii. Pour the mix into the prepared pan (it will look like a lot).

Evenly distribute the mixture and press firmly into the pan. Bake on the bottom shelf of the oven for 20 to 25 minutes until beginning to brown. It should be completely baked through.

Assembly
Best Caramel Ever
Baked Shortbread Base

3   ounces semisweet chocolate (85 grams)

2   teaspoons shortening

4   ounces toffee bits* (114 grams)

*Hershey's Heath Bits o'Brickle Toffee Bits can be found in most grocery stores usually with the chocolate chips and other add ins. Another brand is Skor's Toffee Bits.

Spread the caramel evenly over the baked shortbread base. Melt the chocolate and shortening together over a double broiler or in the microwave at half power. Whisk gently to smooth and combine. Spread the melted chocolate evenly over the caramel. Immediately sprinkle the toffee bits over the chocolate, pressing in lightly.

Refrigerate for 10 to 15 minutes to set. Cut 5 across and 3 or 4 down.

Yield: 15 to 20 bars

Storage: These bars will keep at room temperature in a closed container for five days or so if the room is cool. If the room is too warm, store in the refrigerator but bring to room temperature to serve. They can also be frozen and thawed in the refrigerator before bringing to room temperature to serve. ◆

No-Bake Peanut Butter Bars

These No-Bake Peanut Butter Bars are quickly put together, and just as quickly eaten. These are great to take on a picnic, or to serve as dessert at an outdoor dinner. If you love peanut butter cups, these are a bigger and better version. These No-Bake Peanut Butter Bars fall into the "ridiculously easy" category, and are perfect as something to do with the kids.

Chocolate Crumb Crust

1⅓   cups graham cracker crumbs* (170 grams or 6 ounces)

¼   cup cocoa (25 grams or 1 scant ounce)

½   cup powdered sugar (55 grams or 2 ounces)

½   cup unsalted butter, melted (114 grams, 4 ounces, or 1 stick)

*Buy in crumb form or run graham crackers through a food processor.

Line an 8x8x2 inch pan with parchment paper.

Combine the graham cracker crumbs, cocoa, and powdered sugar in a bowl. Mix very well. Pour the melted butter on top and mix with a fork until completely combined. Press the crumbs into the bottom of the pan. Set aside.

Peanut Butter Filling

1½   cups creamy peanut butter* (340 grams or 12 ounces)

½   cup unsalted butter, very very soft but not runny (114 grams, 4 ounces, or 1 stick)

3½   cups powdered sugar (454 grams or 1 pound)

2   teaspoons vanilla extract

¼   cup heavy cream

*Commercial peanut butter such as Jif or Peter Pan works best.

Combine all ingredients in the bowl of a mixer. Beat until completely combined. Spread over the chocolate crust using an offset spatula.

Chocolate Ganache

½   cup heavy cream

2   tablespoons clear corn syrup

5   tablespoons unsalted butter (75 grams, 2⅔

ounces, ½ stick + 1 tablespoon)

10   ounces semisweet chocolate, finely chopped
(285 grams)

Combine the cream, corn syrup, and butter in a small saucepan. Heat until the butter melts and is steaming hot, but do not let it boil. Remove from the heat, and submerge the chocolate. Wait several minutes, then whisk gently until smooth. Spread over the peanut butter filling. Chill until set.

Release bars by turning the pan upside down onto a cake board. Use a blow dryer set on high to heat the edges of the pan until the bars drop out (see page xxxix for technique). Remove the parchment paper and turn right side up. Cut 4 across and 3 down.

Yield: 12 bars

Storage: These will keep for several days stored in a closed container at room temperature if the room is cool. For longer storage, these will last 5 to 7 days covered in the refrigerator (if they are hidden from everyone)! Serve at room temperature. ◆

Banana Split Bars

THESE BARS ARE A BY-PRODUCT of and a tribute to my love for banana splits. My father owned a drugstore with an ice cream counter when I was young. My right arm developed quite the muscle tone from scooping hard ice cream. There was just something special about that long glass dish made especially for a banana cut lengthwise. Three scoops of ice cream featuring a different topping for each, finished with whipped cream, a sprinkling of nuts, and a maraschino cherry with the stem left on, was my absolute favorite.

These bars have all the flavors of a banana split (but they won't melt)!

Banana Split Bars

1½   cups pureed bananas, about 3 large bananas

2   cups all-purpose flour (280 grams or 10 ounces)

½   teaspoon salt

1   teaspoon baking soda

1½   cups granulated sugar (300 grams or 3½ ounces)

½   cup unsalted butter, softened (114 grams, 4 ounces, or 1 stick)

1   tablespoon vanilla extract

2   large eggs
1   cup sour cream (225 grams or 8 ounces)
½   cup chocolate chips (85 grams or 3 ounces)
½   cup pecan pieces (60 grams or 2 ounces)
½   cup drained maraschino cherries, halved (85 grams or 3 ounces)

Preheat the oven to 350°F / 175°C. Line a 10x15 inch jelly roll pan with parchment paper. Spray the paper and sides of the pan with a non-stick baking release. Set aside.

Peel the bananas and puree in a blender or food processor. Measure 1½ cups. Set aside.

Whisk the flour, salt, and baking soda together. Set aside.

Cream the sugar, butter, and vanilla in a mixing bowl until light. Scrape down the sides of the bowl and add the eggs and sour cream. The mixture may curdle at this point, but that is fine.

Mix in the bananas, followed by the dry ingredients, scraping down the sides of the bowl several times to mix completely. The batter will be very thick. Add the chocolate chips, pecans, and cherries.

Spread evenly in the prepared pan, and bake for 22 to 24 minutes until a cake tester comes out clean. Cool on a rack, release, and finish as below.

Pineapple Buttercream

1   8-ounce can of crushed pineapple in juice
¾   cup unsalted butter, softened (170 grams, 6 ounces, or 1½ sticks)
2⅓   cups powdered sugar (300 grams or 10½ ounces)
1   tablespoon vanilla extract
2-3 teaspoons milk if needed

Drain the pineapple very well. Squeeze it between your hands until completely dry. Set aside.

Combine the butter, powdered sugar, and vanilla in a mixing bowl. Beat on low speed until it comes together. Raise the speed to medium, and beat until very light and the volume has increased. Blend in the pineapple. Add the milk, a little at a time, if needed to obtain a spreadable consistency. Spread evenly over the banana cake.

Finishing the Banana Split Bars

½   cup chopped pecans (60 grams or 2 ounces)
3   ounces semisweet chocolate (85 grams)
1   teaspoon shortening
30   maraschino cherry halves

Immediately after frosting, sprinkle with the chopped pecans.

Melt the chocolate and shortening together over a double broiler or in the microwave at half power. Using a spoon, drizzle the chocolate over the pecans. Refrigerate to firm the chocolate and buttercream.

When set, cut 6 across and 5 down. Let the bars come to room temperature, and press a cherry half into the middle of each bar.

Yield: 30 bars

Storage: These will keep at room temperature for several days. Refrigerate for longer storage or freeze. Thaw at room temperature. ◆

Cheesecake Bars

NOT ONLY ARE THESE CHEESECAKE Bars easy, but they are also extremely versatile. The basic cheesecake can be turned into lemon, lime, lemon-lime, raspberry, or lemon-raspberry with little to no trouble. Cut the bars in half and you have a great addition to a cookie or petit four tray.

Cheesecake Bars Base

¾   cup unsalted butter, cold and cut into small pieces (170 grams, 6 ounces, or 1½ sticks)

1¼   cups all-purpose flour (170 grams or 6 ounces)

⅓   cup + 1 tablespoon granulated sugar (78 grams or about 2¾ ounces)

2   large egg yolks

Preheat the oven to 350°F / 175°C. Spray the bottom of a 9x13x2 inch pan with a non-stick baking release. Line with parchment paper and spray the entire pan.

Combine the butter and flour in the bowl of a processor. Process until it forms a powder.

Add the sugar and process to mix completely. Add the egg yolks and process until a ball forms. Redistribute the dough if it doesn't want to come together (see Press in Crusts, page xxxvi).

Press into the bottom of the pan as evenly as possible. Bake for 25 minutes until golden brown.

Using a spoon, press the crust against the sides of the pan so that the crust fits snuggly with no spaces (see page xxxvi for technique).

Filling

1½   pounds cream cheese, room temperature (680 grams or 3 8-ounce packages)

1   cup + 2 tablespoons granulated sugar (225 grams or 8 ounces)

1   tablespoon cornstarch

3   large eggs

¼   cup heavy cream

1   tablespoon vanilla extract

Without cleaning the processor bowl, break the cream cheese into 4 to 6 pieces, distributing them evenly around the bowl. Pour the sugar and cornstarch over the cream cheese. Process until completely smooth, scraping the sides of the bowl often.

Add the eggs, heavy cream, and vanilla, processing until smooth with no lumps. Scrape often.

Pour mixture over the baked crust. Bake for 30 to 35 minutes until the filling is set. The sides may rise slightly, but they will fall as it cools. The top should remain colorless. Cool for about 15 minutes, then loosen the edges with a metal spatula. Leave in the pan.

Place in the refrigerator overnight when fully cooled.

Loosen the edges again with a straight metal spatula. Turn the cheesecake out onto a cake board. Remove the parchment paper and turn right side up. Cut 5 across and 4 down or any size you wish.

Yield: 20 bars

Storage: These store for about 5 days well-covered in the refrigerator. For longer storage, freeze, wrap, and store in the freezer for several months. Thaw in the refrigerator. These can sit at room temperature for hours when ready to serve.

Variations – The base remains the same for all bars. All are baked as above.

Lemon Cheesecake Bars – Add the zest of one large lemon, and substitute ¼ cup lemon juice for the cream. Omit the vanilla extract.

Lime Cheesecake Bars – Add 2 to 3 teaspoons lime zest, and substitute ¼ cup freshly squeezed lime juice for the cream.

Lemon-Lime Cheesecake Bars - Add the zest of half a large lemon, and about 2 teaspoons of lime zest. Use half lemon and half lime juice in place of the cream (⅛ cup each).

Raspberry Cheesecake Bars – Cool the crust completely. If the raspberry jam is stiff, stir to loosen. Spread ½ cup of jam to within ½" of the edges over the cooled crust. Pour the filling over the jam.

Lemon-Raspberry Cheesecake Bars – Cool the crust completely. Spread ½ cup raspberry jam over the crust as in the Raspberry Cheesecake Bars. Make the Lemon Cheesecake Bars and pour over the jam. ◆

Pecan Bars

THESE PECAN BARS ARE ONE of the most popular recipes from the Culinary Institute of America. They called them Pecan Diamonds because of the shape in which they were cut. I have seen many versions of these Pecan Bars, but this is the recipe we used at the bakery. The key is to boil the syrup for the filling to a temperature of 240°F / 116°C, or the soft-ball stage. If the filling is undercooked it will sag when cut. If it is overcooked, it will be too hard and very difficult to eat.

Pecan Bars Base

1¼   cups all-purpose flour (170 grams or 6 ounces)

¾   cup unsalted butter* (170 grams, 6 ounces, or 1½ sticks)

⅓   cup granulated sugar (65 grams or 2¼ ounces)

2   large egg yolks

*Cold and cut into small pieces for the processor method. Softened for the mixer method.

Preheat the oven to 325°F / 163°C. Line the bottom of a 9x13x2 inch pan with parchment paper and spray with non-stick baking release. Set aside.

Processor Method

The butter should be cold and cut into small pieces for this method. Place the flour in the bowl of a processor, and place the butter on top. Process until the butter is indistinguishable. Add the sugar and pulse in. Add the egg yolks and process until a dough forms.

Mixer Method

The butter should be softened for this method. Place the flour, butter, and sugar in the bowl of a mixer fitted with the paddle attachment. Cut in the butter until mealy. Add the egg yolks and mix together until a dough forms.

Pressing in the Crust – See page xxxviii.

Break the dough into pieces and distribute them in the prepared pan. Press in evenly.

Making sure there are no visable seams where the pieces meet.

Bake 15 to 20 minutes until golden brown.

Immediately after removing from the oven, use the back of a spoon to press the crust firmly against the sides of the pan to seal. Cool the crust to lukewarm. While the crust is cooling, make the filling.

Pecan Filling

1   cup unsalted butter (225 grams, 8 ounces, or 2 sticks)

½   cup honey (170 grams or 6 ounces)

¼   cup granulated sugar (50 grams or 1¾ ounce)

1   cup + 2 tablespoons packed light brown sugar (225 grams or 8 ounces)

¼   cup heavy cream

1¼   pounds chopped pecans (565 grams – approx. 5½ cups)

Melt together the butter, honey, both sugars, and cream in a large saucepan. Bring to a boil and cook to 240°F / 116°C (soft-ball stage).

Remove mixture from the heat, and immediately stir in the pecans.

Quickly pour over the base, and smooth with an offset spatula.

Bake for exactly 25 minutes. It will be bubbly around the edges and look unset - That is how it should be. Cool completely.

Release from the pan using a blow dryer set on high (see page xxxix). Place a cake board over the top of the pan, and turn it upside down. Remove the parchment paper. Trim the edges while upside down.

Turn right side up and cut 6 across and 4 down.

Yield: 24 bars

Storage: These keep for a week in an airtight container. For longer storage, freeze and thaw in the refrigerator. Serve and keep at room temperature. ◆

Chocolate Raspberry Squares

THE BASE FOR THESE SQUARES originally was a stand-alone cake, but I loved it so much I used it as a base for items from the bakery. Its intense chocolate flavor has the ability to enhance an endless number of toppings.

Small or large, bar cookie or cake, this moist and chocolatey Reine de Saba base is the perfect foil for the tart raspberry jam.

The one caveat is to make sure you don't overbake it because it will dry out. Also, this recipe has an unusual method of adding the eggs, but we have found this to be the best procedure to ensure a flat layer.

Chocolate Raspberry Squares Base

½   cup all-purpose flour (70 grams or 2½ ounces)
½   teaspoon baking soda
8   ounces semisweet chocolate (225 grams)
1   cup unsalted butter, softened (225 grams, 8 ounces, or 2 sticks)

½ cup granulated sugar (100 grams or 3½ ounces)
4 large eggs

Preheat the oven to 350°F / 175°C. Line a 9x13x2 inch pan with parchment paper. Spray the entire pan with non-stick baking release.

Combine the flour and baking soda. Set aside.

Melt the chocolate over a double boiler or in the microwave at half power. Set aside to cool to lukewarm.

Please note that all beating for this recipe should be on low speed, and only as long as necessary to combine. There should be no air beaten into the mixture.

Beat the butter and sugar on low speed until well combined. Scrape down the sides of the bowl. Add 2 eggs and beat well. The mixture may curdle, but continue anyway.

Add the melted chocolate and mix on low speed until fully blended. Scrape the bowl often. Add the remaining 2 eggs and beat to combine. Add the flour mixture and mix on low speed, scraping several times to fully incorporate. Spread dough evenly in the prepared pan.

Bake for 18 to 20 minutes until a cake tester comes out clean. Do not overbake or it will be dry.

Cool completely. The base can be wrapped and refrigerated for several days or frozen for a month.

Butter Glaze
½ cup butter (114 grams, 4 ounces, or 1 stick)
6 ounces semisweet chocolate (170 grams)

Melt the butter and chocolate over a double broiler or in the microwave at half power. Do not let the mixture get too hot. Use immediately.

Finishing
Baked base, cooled
⅓ cup seedless red raspberry jam
Butter glaze
Fresh raspberries, optional

Spread the jam over the cooled base layer. Pour the glaze on top and spread evenly. Chill until just set enough to cut.

Trim edges and cut 4 across and 5 down. Top each square with a fresh raspberry.

Yield: 20 squares

Storage: If fresh raspberries were used, these may be stored in a closed container at room temperature for a day. After that they should be refrigerated. If no fresh raspberries were used, these may be stored well-covered for several days at room temperature. These freeze well without the fresh raspberries. Thaw in the refrigerator and serve at room temperature. ◆

Dutch Apple Crumb Bars

A SIMPLE PRESS-IN SHORTBREAD CRUST is covered with apples, sugar, spices, and brandy, then topped with Dutch apple crumbs for an unusual bar cookie. As if that weren't enough, the finishing touch is an easy caramel drizzle or a dusting of powdered sugar.

It will seem like there are a lot of apples in this recipe; however, as they bake, they become soft and compact. The finished bars will not be as tall as they are when they go into the oven.

Crumb Topping
½   cup unsalted butter, softened (114 grams, 4 ounces, or 1 stick)
⅔   cup packed light or dark brown sugar (130 grams or about 4½ ounces)
½   teaspoon cinnamon
½   teaspoon nutmeg
¼   teaspoon salt
1½ cup cake flour (190 grams or about 6⅔ ounces)

Beat the butter and brown sugar in a mixing bowl until very light and fluffy.

Whisk together the dry ingredients, and add them to the butter mixture. Mix on low speed until crumbs start to form, scraping the sides and bottom of the bowl several times. Do not overmix or it will turn into a paste. Refrigerate the crumbs until needed.

Shortbread Crust
1½ cups all-purpose flour (210 grams flour 7⅓ ounces)
½   cup powdered sugar (65 grams or 2¼ ounces)
¾   cup + 1 tablespoon unsalted butter, cold and cut into little pieces (195 grams, about 6¾ ounces, or 13 tablespoons)

Preheat oven to 350°F / 175°C. Line the bottom of a 9x13x2 inch pan with parchment paper. Spray the paper and the sides of the pan with a non-stick baking release.

Combine the flour and powdered sugar in a processor. Process to mix. Add the cold butter and process until indistinguishable.

Pour the mixture into the prepared pan - It will look like a lot (see page xxxvii). Evenly distribute the mixture and press firmly into the pan.

Bake for 20 to 25 minutes on the bottom shelf until beginning to brown.

Apple Filling
6   large apples*
3   tablespoons brandy
⅓   cup all-purpose flour (45 grams or 1½ ounces)
¾   cup granulated sugar (150 grams or 5¼ ounces)
1   teaspoons cinnamon
1   teaspoon nutmeg

*I used 3 Granny Smith and 3 Gala apples for a total of about 3 pounds.

Peel, core, and slice the apples thinly. There should be about 8 cups. Place them in a large bowl with the brandy.

Whisk together the dry ingredients. Add the mixture to the bowl of apples and mix well to fully coat.

Spread evenly over the baked crust. Evenly distribute the crumb topping.

Bake for 45 to 55 minutes until the crumbs are browned and the apples are soft. Tent the pan loosely with foil if the crumbs are browning too quickly.

Cool for about 10 minutes, then release the edges with a metal spatula and cool completely.

Turn the bars out of the pan, then flip them right side up. Refrigerate to firm before finishing and cutting.

Caramel Drizzle Finish – I used Werther's Soft Caramels for this drizzle. Other caramels may be used, but the amount of cream may need to be altered to get to a consistency that drizzles off a spoon.

1   4½-ounce package Werther's Soft Caramels
2   teaspoons heavy cream

Melt the caramels and cream together in the microwave for about 30 seconds. Stir and drizzle over the baked bars. Refrigerate briefly to set the caramel. Cut 4 across and 6 down.

Powdered Sugar Finish – Dust with powdered sugar.

Yield: 24 bars

Storage: These will keep at room temperature for a day or two, then refrigerate. For longer storage, freeze the uncut and unfinished bars. Thaw completely on a rack at room temperature, then drizzle the bars with caramel or dust with powdered sugar as above. ◆

Hawaiian Carrot Cake Squares

ONE OF AMERICA'S MOST POPULAR cakes becomes a tribute to our 50th state featuring favorite flavors from Hawaii. Honey, buttermilk, oil, and pineapple work together to make the moistest carrot cake you will ever eat. Instead of the traditionally used pecans or walnuts, toasted macadamia nuts are added to this batter to complete this Hawaiian treat, the cream cheese frosting is topped with toasted coconut. These squares are sure to be a hit wherever you take them.

Hawaiian Carrot Cake Bars

1 cup macadamia nuts (120 grams or 4¼ ounces)

1½ cups all-purpose flour (210 grams or 7⅓ ounces)

1½ teaspoons cinnamon

¾ teaspoon baking soda

⅓ teaspoon salt

3 large eggs

⅓ cup vegetable oil

½ cup buttermilk

¼ cup honey

1⅓ cups packed brown sugar (265 grams or 9⅓ ounces)

2 cups peeled and shredded carrots (170 grams or 6 ounces)

1 8-ounce can crushed pineapple, drained and squeezed dry (225 grams)

Preheat the oven to 350°F / 175°C. Line the bottom of a 9x13x2 inch pan with parchment paper. Spray the entire pan with a non-stick baking release and set aside.

Place the macadamia nuts on a rimmed baking sheet and toast for about 8 to 10 minutes until medium brown and fragrant. Cool and chop coarsely. Set aside.

Whisk the flour, cinnamon, baking soda, and salt together. Set aside.

Combine the eggs, oil, buttermilk, honey, and brown sugar in the bowl of a mixer fitted with the paddle attachment. Mix on low speed to blend completely.

Add the flour mixture and mix well on low speed. Add the carrots, pineapple, and toasted nuts. Beat on low speed until blended.

Pour the batter into the prepared pan and smooth with a spatula. Bake for 27 to 30 minutes until a cake tester comes out clean. Cool in the pan, then release the cake.

Coconut Cream Cheese Frosting

1½ cups unsweetened coconut (90 grams or 3 ounces)

4 tablespoons unsalted butter, softened (60 grams, 2 ounces, or ½ stick)

6 ounces cream cheese, softened (170 grams)

1 teaspoon vanilla extract

2⅔ cups powdered sugar (340 grams or 12 ounces)

Preheat the oven to 350°F / 175°C. Spread the coconut in a single layer on a rimmed baking sheet. Toast for about 5 to 7 minutes until it starts browning. Watch carefully; unsweetened coconut toasts much faster and more evenly than sweetened coconut. Remove from the oven and stir well. Cool.

Place the butter, cream cheese, and vanilla in a mixing bowl. Beat until completely mixed. Add the powdered sugar and beat on low speed to incorporate. Raise the speed to high and beat to lighten and increase the volume.

Spread frosting over the cooled carrot cake base, and immediately top with the toasted coconut. Lightly press in the coconut. Cut 3 across and 5 down.

Yield: 15 squares

Storage: Keep in a covered container at room temperature for one day, then refrigerate. These will keep for about 5 days if stored in an airtight container. They also freeze well, simply thaw in the refrigerator and serve at room temperature. ◆

Hermit Bars

ONE OF MY SONS AND I absolutely love spiced cookies. He likes a bit of crunch to his cookies, and these bars more than fit the bill. To this day, whenever he visits, these Hermits are waiting for him. These are so easy to make; the only caveat is not to overbake them.

If you look closely at the photo, you will see that some of the bars are decorated with edible confetti and some are not. I was once informed that the decorations were a welcomed crunch factor. Needless to say, I haven't left them off since. Sometimes I use the multi colored nonpareils, which are even crunchier, so I'm told. We won't discuss who was telling me this!

Hermit Bars

2	cups all-purpose flour (280 grams or 10 ounces)
¾	teaspoon baking soda
½	teaspoon baking powder
1	teaspoon ground ginger
1	teaspoon coarse ground black pepper
1	teaspoon cinnamon
½	teaspoon cloves
½	teaspoon nutmeg
¼	teaspoon salt
½	cup unsalted butter, softened (114 grams, 4 ounces, or 1 stick)
1	cup packed light or dark brown sugar (200 grams or 7 ounces)
2	large eggs
⅓	cup light molasses

Preheat the oven to 350°F / 175°C. Line the bottom of a 9x13x2 inch pan or a quarter sheet pan with parchment paper. Spray the parchment paper and the sides of the pan with a non-stick baking release.

Whisk together the flour, baking soda, baking powder, ginger, black pepper, cinnamon, cloves, nutmeg, and salt. Set aside.

Cream together the butter and brown sugar until light and fluffy. Add the eggs and mix in completely. Add the molasses, and beat until combined. If the mixture appears curdled, raise the speed and mix until it comes together. Don't worry if it doesn't, it will when the flour is added.

Add the flour mixture and mix on low speed until fully incorporated. Scrape the sides of the bowl often.

Scrape into the prepared pan and smooth with an offset spatula. Because this is a very sticky batter, I recommend using a damp spatula. I take my pan over to the sink area, run cold water on the spatula, shake to remove excess water, and then use it to spread the batter. Repeat wetting the spatula as often as necessary to completely smooth and even it out. Alternatively, you can wet the palm of your hand and use it to smooth the batter.

Bake for 18 to 20 minutes. Do not overbake. A tester should come out slightly moist. The edges of the cookies will be higher than the center when they are done. **Immediately flatten the edges with an offset spatula.** Cool completely.

To release, loosen the edges with a spatula and turn out the Hermits. Leave them upside down.

Lemon Glaze

3   to 4 tablespoons lemon juice
2   cups powdered sugar (260 grams or 9⅛ ounces)
    Multicolored sprinkles or confetti, optional

Starting with 3 tablespoons of lemon juice, stir the powdered sugar and lemon juice together to create a glaze. If the glaze is too thick, add lemon juice a little at a time to thin it out.

Turn the Hermits right side up and spread the lemon glaze on top. Scatter the sprinkles or confetti if you desire (remember the recommendation above). Let the glaze dry – this may take 4 to 5 hours or longer if it is humid.

Trim the edges. Cut 5 or 6 across and 4 down.

Yield: 20 to 24 bars

Storage: Store in an airtight container for about 5 days. They can also be frozen whole without the glaze. Thaw at room temperature, then glaze and cut. ◆

Almond Raspberry Triangles

ALMOND RASPBERRY TRIANGLES WERE ONE of the most popular petit fours in our petit four box. These are a very easy-to-make cookie, featuring a shortbread base topped with raspberry jam and finished with an amaretto-enhanced almond topping.

The processor makes quick work of both the base and the topping. The versatility of this treat makes them a must-have in a cookie repertoire. They can be cookies, bars, triangles, or petit fours. They served many purposes at the bakery depending on what we needed. As an added bonus, they ship and travel well.

Base for Almond Raspberry Triangles

1½   cups all-purpose flour (210 grams or 7⅓ ounces)
½   cup + 2 tablespoons unsalted butter* (140 grams, 5 ounces, or 1¼ sticks)
⅓   cup granulated sugar (65 grams or 2¼ ounces)
½   cup seedless red raspberry jam

*The butter should be cold and cut into small pieces for the processor method. Softened for the mixer method.

Preheat the oven to 350°F / 175°C. Line a quarter sheet pan or a 9x13x2 inch pan with foil, being sure to also cover the sides of the pan. Spray well with a non-stick baking release and set aside.

Processor Method – Butter should be cold and cut into small pieces. Place the flour in the processor bowl. Add the cold butter and process until indistinguishable. Add the sugar and process. It will be very powdery, see page xxxvii.

Mixer Method – Butter should be softened. Cream the butter and sugar until light. Add the flour, and beat until completely mixed. It should form crumbs.

Turn the dough into the prepared pan, and spread it out evenly. Press in firmly to compact and completely cover the bottom of the pan.

Bake for 22 to 25 minutes until medium brown and completely baked.

As soon as it comes out of the oven, use the back of a spoon to press the base firmly against the sides of the pan to fill any gaps (see page xxxvii) ensuring that the dough adheres to the sides of the pan so the filling does not leak under the baked base.

Spread the raspberry jam over the baked base and set aside.

Topping
6   ounces almonds (170 grams)
¾   cup granulated sugar (150 grams or 5⅓ ounces)

2   large eggs
1   large egg white
¼   teaspoon salt
2   tablespoons Amaretto*
1   teaspoon vanilla extract
1   teaspoon almond extract
4   tablespoons unsalted butter, melted (60 grams, 2 ounces, or ½ stick)
     Powdered sugar for dusting, optional

*Small single-serving bottles of Amaretto (or any similar Almond Liqueur) can be purchased in grocery stores or liquor stores. I believe the almond liqueur gives these Almond Raspberry Triangles a distinct flavor. If you wish to omit it, increase the almond extract to 2 teaspoons and add 1½ tablespoons water in place of the liqueur.

Spread the almonds in a single layer on a baking sheet. Toast them at 350°F / 175°C for 8 to 10 minutes until lightly browned and fragrant. Cool completely before continuing.

Process the almonds and sugar until finely ground. Add the rest of the ingredients and process until completely combined. Pour the mixture over the raspberry jam.

Place the pan on a half sheet pan to make it easier to get it in and out of the oven. Bake 25 to 30 minutes until golden brown and set. Cool.

The jam will stick to the foil when baked. To facilitate removing the foil, chill or freeze the Almond Raspberry Triangles until very cold. Turn upside down and remove the foil, being careful around the edges. Turn right side up.

Cut 4 across and 5 down to make 20 squares. Cut each square diagonally for 40 triangles. Dust with powdered sugar before serving.

Yield: 20 squares or 40 triangles

Storage: These keep well stored in a closed container for 5 or 6 days. The cut, baked triangles will keep for several months well-wrapped in the freezer. ◆

Lemon Bars Updated

LEMON BARS ARE AS AMERICAN as chocolate chip cookies, and loved just as much. In fact, lemon is the second favorite flavor in America, just behind chocolate.

The recipe for my lemon bars came from my first copy of the Betty Crocker Cookbook, which I still have! It was given to me when I got married. With that recipe, however, I found that sometimes the crust would pull away slightly from the sides, allowing the liquid filling to seep underneath. To avoid this, see page xxxvii.

For some reason, instead of granulated sugar, I decided to use powdered sugar. This is also called confectioner's sugar or 10x sugar. In Great Britain it is called icing sugar, and in France, sucre glace. No matter the name, it is all granulated sugar that has

been very finely ground into a powder. It also contains 3% cornstarch to keep it from clumping.

I am not sure if it is the fineness of the sugar that instantly dissolves in the lemon juice and eggs, or the cornstarch helping to bind the filling, but these are the best lemon bars I have ever made. When I used granulated sugar, I would see a heavy sludge of sugar and lemon juice at the bottom of the processor bowl. Now I don't. The filling is much smoother and when you taste it, there is not a single grain of sugar to be found. Since lemon bars have such a sugar-heavy filling, this one change made a world of difference.

Lemon Bar Base

1⅔   cups all-purpose flour (225 grams or 8 ounces)

¼   cup powdered sugar (30 grams or 1 ounce)

⅞   cup unsalted butter, cold and cut into small pieces (200 grams, 7 ounces, or 14 tablespoons)

Preheat the oven to 350°F /175°C. Line the bottom of a 9x13x2 inch pan or quarter sheet pan with parchment paper. Spray the paper and sides of the pan with a non-stick baking release. Set aside.

Combine the flour and powdered sugar in the bowl of a processor. Process to mix. Add the cold butter and process until indistinguishable and powdery. Do not overprocess to make a dough. See Press in Crusts xxxvii.

Evenly distribute the crumbs and press firmly into the bottom of the pan. Bake on the bottom shelf of the oven for 25 minutes until medium brown and baked through. Immediately upon removing from the oven, press the crust against the sides of the pan with the back of a spoon (see page xxxvii for technique).

Lemon Bar Filling

3   cups powdered sugar (390 grams or 13⅔ ounces)

¼   cup all-purpose flour (35 grams or about 1¼ ounces)

½   teaspoon baking powder

4   large eggs + 1 large yolk

½   cup lemon juice, freshly squeezed

Combine the powdered sugar, flour, and baking powder in the processor bowl (no need to clean it). Process to mix. Add the eggs, yolk, and lemon juice processing just to blend completely.

Pour the filling over the baked crust. If using a quarter sheet pan, it is safest to place it inside a half sheet pan as it will be very full.

Carefully place in the oven on the middle shelf. Bake 25 minutes or just until set. Cool. Chill for several hours.

Release the bars by going around the edges with a small metal spatula. Turn out onto a cake board, remove the parchment paper, and turn right side up. Cut 6 across and 4 down. After cutting, let the bars come to room temperature and sprinkle with powdered sugar.

Yield: 24 bars

Storage: Keep in a covered container at room temperature for several days. Refrigerate or freeze for longer storage. If freezing, do not dust with powdered sugar until thawed and brought to room temperature. ◆

Chocolate Cheesecake Bars

A SIMPLE CHOCOLATE GRAHAM CRACKER crust is topped with a creamy chocolate cheesecake. The processor makes this a snap to put together quickly. A chocolate-raspberry version is also easy to make.

Chocolate Cheesecake Bars Crumb Crust

½   cup + 1 tablespoon unsalted butter (135 grams, about 4¾ ounces, or 1 stick + 1 tablespoon)

½   cup powdered sugar (65 grams or 2¼ ounces)

⅓   cup cocoa, Dutch or natural (30 grams or 1 ounce)

1½   cups graham cracker crumbs (170 grams 6 ounces)

Preheat the oven to 350°F / 175°C. Line the bottom of a 9x13x2 inch pan with parchment paper and spray with a non-stick baking release. Set aside.

Melt the butter and set aside.

In a large bowl, sift the powdered sugar and cocoa together. Whisk in the graham cracker crumbs. Add the melted butter and mix with a fork making sure all the crumbs are coated. I usually finish mixing by hand.

Pour into the prepared pan, distribute evenly, and firmly press in the crust. Set aside.

Chocolate Cheesecake Filling

5   ounces semisweet chocolate (140 grams)
1½ pounds cream cheese, room temperature (680 grams, 24 ounces, or 3 8-ounce packages)
1   cup + 2 tablespoons granulated sugar (225 grams or 8 ounces)
1   tablespoon cornstarch
3   large eggs
1   tablespoon vanilla extract

Melt the chocolate in a double boiler or in the microwave at half power. Set aside to cool to lukewarm.

Place the cream cheese, sugar, and cornstarch in the bowl of a food processor. Process until perfectly smooth, scraping the sides several times.

Add the eggs and vanilla, and process to mix. Add the melted chocolate and process to mix completely, scraping several times.

Pour over the crust. Bake 35 to 40 minutes until set.

Cool until lukewarm. Release the edges with a small metal spatula. Leaving the cheesecake in the pan, chill until cold.

Go around the edges again and release the cheesecake by turning it upside down onto a cake board or tray. Turn it right side up. Cut 5 across and 4 down.

Chocolate-Raspberry Cheesecake Bars - Spread ½ cup raspberry jam on the top of the crust. Add the cheesecake topping and continue as above.

Yield: 20 bars

Storage: Cover and store in the refrigerator for several days, or freeze well-wrapped for several months. Thaw in the refrigerator and serve at room temperature. ◆

Evelyn's Chewy Peanut Butter Bars

THE FRAMEWORK FOR THIS RECIPE was given to me many years ago by my sister-in-law, Evelyn. They were great then and just as great now. The heading read, "A quickly-made treat for a snack, sack lunch, or a meal." True then and true now, but we call it brown bagging for lunch now.

Commercial peanut butter such as Jif or Peter Pan works best in this recipe.

Chewy Peanut Butter Bars

1   cup all-purpose flour (140 grams or 5 ounces)

1   teaspoon baking powder

¼   teaspoon salt

⅓   cup unsalted butter, softened (75 grams, 2⅔ ounces, or ½ stick + 1 tablespoon)

½   cup peanut butter (125 grams or 4⅓ ounces)

¼   cup packed light or dark brown sugar (50 grams or 1¾ ounces)

1   cup granulated sugar (200 grams or 7 ounces)

2   large eggs

1   teaspoon vanilla extract

1⅓   cups sweetened shredded coconut (100 grams or 3½ ounces)

Preheat the oven to 350°F / 175°C. Line a 9x13x2 inch pan with parchment paper. Spray the paper and sides of the pan with a non-stick baking release. Set aside.

Whisk the flour, baking powder, and salt together. Set aside.

Cream the butter, peanut butter, and both sugars until light and fluffy. Add the eggs and vanilla, beating well. Add the flour mixture, mixing on low speed just to combine. Finally, add the coconut.

Spread evenly into the prepared pan. Bake for 20 to 23 minutes until a tester comes out clean. Do not overbake or they will be dry. Cool completely before releasing.

Cut 5 across and 4 down.

Yield: 20 bars

Storage: These keep well in an airtight container for about 5 days. They can also be frozen well-wrapped for several months. ♦

Lemon-Steeped Gingerbread Squares

I CAN SCARCELY BELIEVE THIS, but when I was young, my entire family was concerned because I wouldn't eat. Boy, did I do a turnaround on that! My mother could always depend on something sweet to entice me to eat. To that end, dessert was offered every evening after dinner. One of my favorites was gingerbread cake with a warm lemon sauce.

This flavorful treat only requires a few measuring tools, a bowl, a whisk, and a small saucepan. These bars literally come together in minutes.

Lemon-Steeped Gingerbread Squares

1¼ cups all-purpose flour (175 grams or about 6⅛ ounces)
2 teaspoons cinnamon
1 teaspoon ginger
½ teaspoon nutmeg
¼ teaspoon cloves
½ teaspoon baking soda

½ cup mild-flavored or light molasses*
½ cup granulated sugar (100 grams or 3½ ounces)
½ cup unsalted butter, melted (114 grams, 4 ounces, or 1 stick)
½ cup buttermilk
1 large egg

*I like to use Grandma's Molasses because it doesn't use sulfur when it is manufactured.

Preheat the oven to 350°F / 175°C. Line the bottom of an 8x8x2 inch square pan with parchment paper. Spray the entire pan with a non-stick baking release.

Whisk together the flour, spices, and baking soda.

In a large bowl, whisk together the molasses, sugar, melted butter, buttermilk, and egg. Whisk in the dry ingredients and pour into the prepared pan.

Bake for about 25 minutes or until a tester comes out clean. Cool for 10 minutes.

Lemon Soaking Syrup
Prepare while the cake is baking.

¼ cup lemon juice, freshly squeezed
½ cup granulated sugar (100 grams or 3½ ounces)
3 tablespoons unsalted butter (45 grams or 1½ ounces)
Powdered sugar, as needed

Combine the lemon juice, sugar, and butter in a small saucepan and bring to a boil. Set aside but keep warm.

When the gingerbread cake has cooled for 10 minutes, use a wooden skewer to poke holes all over the cake. The holes should not go all the way through to the bottom. Spoon half of the syrup over. After that has soaked in, spoon the remainder of the syrup over the cake. Cool completely.

Release from the pan, turn right side up, and cut 4 across and 4 down. When ready to serve, dust lightly with powdered sugar.

Yield: 16 pieces

Storage: The squares can be kept in a covered container at room temperature for several days. For longer storage, cover and refrigerate or wrap and freeze. Thaw in the refrigerator and serve at room temperature freshly dusted with powdered sugar. ◆

Pecan Pie Squares

IF YOU LIKE PECAN PIE, this is your cookie. The only caveat here is to cut these fairly small because they are very rich. On the other hand… you only live once!

Pecan Pie Squares Base

1¼ cup all-purpose flour (170 grams or 6 ounces)

¾ cup unsalted butter, cold and cut into small pieces (170 grams, 6 ounces, or 1½ sticks)

⅓ cup granulated sugar (65 gram's sugar or 2¼ ounces)

2 large egg yolks

Preheat the oven to 325°F / 163°C. Line the bottom of a 9x13x2 inch pan with parchment paper, and spray with a non-stick baking release. Set aside.

Place the flour in the bowl of a processor. Place the cold butter over the flour, and process until the butter is indistinguishable. Add the sugar and pulse in. Add the egg yolks and process until a dough forms.

Press the dough into the pan as evenly as possible (see page xxxviii for technique). Bake for 20 to 25 minutes until golden brown and almost baked through.

Filling

1 cup packed light or dark brown sugar (200 grams or 7 ounces)

1 cup light corn syrup

½ cup unsalted butter (114 grams, 4 ounces, or 1 stick)

¾ teaspoon salt

4 large eggs, beaten

2½ cups chopped pecans (285 grams or 10 ounces)

2 teaspoons vanilla extract

Combine the brown sugar, corn syrup, and butter in a saucepan. Bring to a boil over medium heat, stirring constantly. Remove from the heat.

Gradually stir a cup of the hot mixture into the beaten eggs. Then, add this back into the mixture in the saucepan. Stir in the pecans and vanilla. Pour the mixture over the baked crust.

Bake for 28 to 32 minutes until the filling is set. Cool in the pan. Cut 5 across and 7 down.

Yield: 35 small squares

Storage: These may be kept in a closed container at room temperature for several days. Refrigerate for longer storage, but bring to room temperature to serve. These also can be frozen well-wrapped - Simply thaw, while still wrapped, in the refrigerator and serve at room temperature. ◆

(Almost) S'Mores Bars

SOME OF US CAN'T WAIT for campfire weather, so here is a bar cookie version of the beloved S'Mores that can be served any time the craving hits. This is a fast and easy recipe that you'll want to keep handy. I know traditional S'Mores don't include peanuts, but you'll be surprised at what a great addition they are.

S'Mores Crust

2	cups graham cracker crumbs (210 grams or 7 ounces)
½	cup powdered sugar (65 grams or 2¼ ounces)
⅔	cup unsalted butter, melted (150 grams, 5⅓ ounces, or 1 stick + 2 tablespoons)
1	teaspoon vanilla extract

Preheat the oven to 350°F / 175°C. Line a 9x13x2 inch pan with parchment paper and spray the entire pan and paper with non-stick baking release. Set aside.

Place the graham cracker crumbs and powdered sugar together in a bowl. Using your hand, squeeze them together to eliminate any lumps, mixing well. Add the butter and toss with a fork or use your hand to fully incorporate.

Distribute the crumbs evenly in the bottom of the prepared pan and press in firmly. Bake for about 12 minutes until medium brown. Remove from the oven and cool completely in the pan. Turn off the oven as you won't need it anymore.

S'Mores Filling

1	cup peanuts, roasted and salted (140 grams or 5 ounces)
2½	cups mini marshmallows (140 grams or 5 ounces)
¾	cup heavy cream
1	pound milk chocolate, coarsely chopped*

*There are lots of good milk chocolates on the market, but one of my favorites is Trader Joe's Pound Plus Milk Chocolate. It is a Belgium chocolate. I can't keep it in the house because I will eat it too fast. Be warned!

Sprinkle the peanuts evenly over the cooled crust. Distribute the marshmallows over the peanuts.

In a saucepan, heat the cream until steamy, but do not boil. Submerge the chocolate in the cream and allow it to sit for a few minutes. Whisk gently to combine. Be careful not to whisk too enthusiastically or the finished S'Mores will have air bubbles in the chocolate.

Pour the chocolate ganache over the marshmallows. If any marshmallows pop up, push them under the chocolate. Refrigerate to set up.

Turn the pan upside down on a cake board. Using a blow dryer on high (see page xxxix for technique), go around the outside edge of the pan *briefly* to soften the chocolate and crust. Pick up the board and pan together and bang it on the counter. Do this on each side of the pan. If the bars don't drop out, reheat briefly and repeat.

Turn them right side up and cut 6 across and 4 down.

Yield: 24 bars

Storage: After the initial chilling, the bars can be kept covered at room temperature for days. If the room is too warm, return to the refrigerator but serve at room temperature. ◆

Triple-Layer Pecan Bars

I USED TO THINK THAT this was the quintessential European cookie; however, I recently realized that the bourbon, pecans, baking soda, and baking powder actually make these a very American bar.

My mother made these every Christmas. She would make the cookies ahead and hide them, but because they were one of my favorites, I could always find them no matter where she stashed them. Every year a few would be missing when she opened the tin, but she never said a word. These are worth every minute they take to make. They are as beautiful as they are delicious.

To make the assembly faster and easier, I roll all the pastry layers between wax paper and freeze them still on the wax paper. The pastry will cling to the paper, making it easy to lower into the pan. After that, it is just a matter of layering.

The pastry layers are very thin, so it is important to use a 10x15 inch jelly roll pan. A half sheet pan will be too big.

Pastry Base

4   large egg yolks

2   tablespoons bourbon*

1   teaspoon vanilla extract

⅓   cup sour cream (75 grams or 2⅔ ounce)

4¼   cups all-purpose flour (595 grams or about 20¾ ounces)

1   tablespoon baking soda

2½   teaspoons baking powder

1¼   cups unsalted butter, cold and cut into small pieces (285 grams, 10 ounces, or 2½ sticks)

1   cup + 2 tablespoons granulated sugar (225 grams or 8 ounces)

*Water may be substituted if necessary, but it will affect the flavor of the pastry.

Whisk together the yolks, bourbon, vanilla, and sour cream. Set aside.

Place the flour, baking soda, and baking powder in the bowl of a food processor. Pulse several times to mix. Add the cold butter and process until the butter is indistinguishable. Add the sugar and pulse to mix. Last, add the liquid ingredient mixture and process.

The mixture will most likely separate into two layers, dough on the bottom and powder on top. Push the powdery layer into the middle of the processor and scrape the sides and bottom of the bowl. Pulse for about 10 seconds, then process until it forms a cohesive mass.

Remove the dough and divide into three parts (420 grams or 14¾ ounces each). If the dough is too soft to roll, refrigerate to firm. Wipe the processor clean.

Filling

1½   pounds pecans, divided (680 grams or 24 ounces)

1   cup granulated sugar, divided (200 grams or 7 ounce)

1½   teaspoons cinnamon, divided

¾   cup seedless red raspberry jam or preserves

¾   cup apricot jam or preserves

1   large egg white

Place ½ pound pecans (225 grams or 8 ounces), ⅓ cup sugar (65 grams or 2¼ ounces), and ½ teaspoon cinnamon in a processor bowl fitted with the steel blade. Process 10 to 15 seconds until the nuts are finely ground. Remove to a bowl. Repeat this twice more keeping each batch in a separate bowl. Set aside. Wipe the processor clean.

Process the apricot preserves to smooth. Set aside.

Stir the raspberry jam to smooth. Set aside.

Assembly

Preheat the oven to 350°F / 175°C. Spray a 10x15 inch jelly roll pan with a non-stick baking release. Line the pan with parchment paper and spray the paper and sides of the pan well. Set aside.

Roll one piece of pastry between wax paper into a 9½ x 14½ inch rectangle (see wax paper technique on page xlii). Still between wax paper, place it on a baking sheet and freeze until hard. Repeat with the remaining two pieces of pastry.

Remove one of the rectangles from the freezer and let it barely begin to soften. Peel off the top piece of parchment paper. Place the pastry in the pan by grasping the bottom piece of paper and turning the dough over into the pan. Peel off the paper.

If the pastry doesn't quite fit, let it soften a bit then trim to fit or gently push the dough into the sides and corners of the pan. Spread the raspberry jam over the pastry.

Pour one portion of the pecan mixture into the center of the pan.

Spread evenly over the jam and press down lightly with your hand.

Place the second piece of pastry over the nuts.

Top with the apricot jam and another portion of the pecan mixture, pressing down lightly.

Place the third piece of pastry over the nuts. Beat the egg white with a fork until very foamy. Using a pastry brush, spread the egg white over the pastry. It is not necessary to use all of it, just make sure the pastry is well covered.

Sprinkle the last portion of the pecan mixture evenly over the egg white. Place a clean piece of wax paper over the nuts and lightly roll over the top several times with a rolling pin.

Bake on the middle rack of the oven for 45 minutes or until a cake tester comes out clean. Cool for about 15 to 20 minutes and release the edges with a small spatula.

Releasing the Bars

Leave the bars in the pan and let them sit at room temperature overnight. Loosen the sides with a spatula again, then place a cake board on top of the pan and turn it upside down onto the board. This will keep the top nuts in place. Remove the parchment paper. Place another board on the bars and flip them right side up.

Trim about ½" off all edges. With a serrated knife, use a sawing motion to get through the top layer and then cut straight down. Cut 9 across and 6 down, wiping the knife clean between each cut.

Yield: 54 bars

Storage: Keep in an airtight container at room temperature for up to 10 days. For longer storage, place in a container with wax paper between layers and freeze for up to 4 months. Defrost the bars on racks at room temperature. ◆

Hazelnut Crunch Bars

THESE HAZELNUT CRUNCH BARS WERE born from one of my fantasies. We once received an order from the Hyatt Hotel for a dessert that had a crunchy base. I never forgot it, and always wanted to incorporate this crunchy cookie into something. With my love of caramel and homemade marshmallow, combining these three with a chocolate ganache topping was the perfect solution. To make these even better, there is no baking involved.

Be sure to make the caramel at least a day or up to a week before making the bars.

Caramel
1   Recipe Best Caramel Ever, cooked to 242°F / 117°C, page xxix

Hazelnut Crunch
½   cup hazelnuts, toasted (60 grams or 2 ounces)
1   cup + 2 tablespoons Rice Krispies cereal (35 grams or 1¼ ounces)
9   ounces milk chocolate (255 grams)

Line a 9x13x2 inch pan with parchment paper. Spray the paper and sides of the pan with a non-stick baking release. Set aside.

Add the cooled, toasted hazelnuts to the bowl of a processor and process until fairly finely ground. Do not overprocess or you will make a paste. Remove them to a large bowl and add the Rice Krispies cereal. Mix well and set aside.

Spray the back of a large spoon with a non-stick baking release and set aside.

Melt the chocolate over a double broiler or in the microwave at half power. Pour it over the hazelnut/cereal mix and quickly mix all of it together with a large spoon or a gloved hand.

Pour into the prepared pan and immediately smooth it with the back of the sprayed spoon or a gloved hand. If it sets up too quickly, place it in the oven on the lowest setting for a few minutes to loosen.

Caramel Layer
Microwave the caramel or heat over a double boiler until spreadable. Do not stir any more than necessary at this point. Pour it over the Hazelnut Crunch layer and spread evenly. Set aside.

Marshmallow
1   tablespoon + 1 teaspoon unflavored gelatin (10 grams, ⅓ ounce, or 1½ envelopes)
¼   cup cold water
3   large egg whites (100 grams or 3½ ounces)
1   teaspoon vanilla extract
½   cup water

1   cup granulated sugar, divided (200 grams or
    7 ounces)
2   tablespoons corn syrup

Sprinkle the gelatin over the ¼ cup cold water. Stir
to moisten all of it. Set aside.

Place the egg whites and vanilla in the bowl of a
mixer. Beat to soft peaks on medium speed. Slowly
add ¼ cup (50 grams or 1⅔ ounces) sugar and beat
to stiff peaks.

As soon as you begin beating the egg whites, combine the water, the remaining ¾ cup of sugar, and
corn syrup in a small saucepan. Bring to a boil,
washing down the sides of the pan with a brush
dipped in cold water.

Boil to a temperature of 240°F / 116°C.

If the egg whites are stiff before the sugar syrup
comes to temperature, lower the speed of the mixer
as low as possible, and keep mixing the whites. **Do
not** turn off the mixer.

As soon as the sugar syrup comes to temperature,
slowly pour it into the mixer bowl. Try to pour the
syrup between the bowl and the whisk so it goes
directly into the egg whites and not onto the whisk
or bowl.

Liquefy the gelatin in the microwave for a few seconds, and pour it over the egg white mixture. Beat
until cold and stiff.

cut 6 across and 4 down with a hot knife. The knife must be dipped in very hot water and quickly dried with a paper towel between each cut. Let the knife melt through the ganache, which will be cold and firm, then cut straight down. This sounds a lot more complicated than it is... You will get into a rhythm and see that it isn't difficult at all to make these very professional-looking cuts.

Yield: 24 bars

Storage: Keep in a closed container at a cool room temperature for a day or two. For longer storage, refrigerate. ◆

If the caramel has hardened, heat the top of the caramel layer with a blow dryer so the marshmallow can adhere to it. Immediately pour the marshmallow over the caramel and smooth it out. Cool completely.

Dark Satin Ganache

½	cup heavy cream
¼	clear corn syrup
5	tablespoons unsalted butter (75 grams, 2⅔ ounces, or ½ stick + 1 tablespoon)
10	ounces semisweet chocolate (285 grams)

Heat the cream, corn syrup, and butter in a small saucepan until steaming hot but not boiling. Submerge the chocolate in the hot cream and let sit for a few minutes. Gently whisk until smooth. Do not whisk too enthusiastically or you will have air bubbles in the ganache (and they are hard to remove). Pour the ganache over the marshmallow and smooth it out. Refrigerate for several hours or overnight.

Loosen the edges with a small flexible spatula and turn out onto a cake board. Turn right side up and

Creamy Lime Bars

THESE BARS ARE A LIME lover's dream. Plenty of lime zest and juice complemented by a cream cheese filling will make these your go-to cookie bar. Not only that, but they are easy to make, look great, and freeze well. You will notice that these are not green. Lime juice is about the same color as lemon juice. I choose not to use green food coloring, but feel free to if you wish.

Creamy Lime Bars Crust

2   cups graham cracker crumbs (210 grams or 7 ounces)
½   cup powdered sugar (65 grams or 2¼ ounces)
⅔   cup unsalted butter, melted (150 grams or 5⅓ ounces, or about 1 stick + 3 tablespoons)
1   teaspoon vanilla extract

Preheat the oven to 350°F / 175°C. Line a 9x13x2 inch pan with parchment paper and spray the entire pan with non-stick baking release. Set aside.

Combine the graham cracker crumbs and powdered sugar in a bowl. Whisk them together to eliminate any lumps. Add the butter and vanilla, and toss with a fork or your hand to mix completely.

Distribute the crumbs evenly in the bottom of the pan. Press in firmly. Bake 10 to 12 minutes until set and lightly browned.

Cream Cheese Filling

     Zest of 1 large lime or 2 smaller ones
8   ounces cream cheese, softened (225 grams)
¼   cup granulated sugar (50 grams or 1¾ ounces)
1   large egg
1   tablespoon milk or cream
1   teaspoon cornstarch
1   teaspoon vanilla extract

Using a microplane grater, zest the lime or limes.

Place all ingredients in the bowl of a food processor and process until smooth. Scrape down the sides often so there are no lumps of cream cheese. Pour the filling over the graham cracker crust and bake for 18 to 22 minutes until this cheesecake layer is completely set.

Lime Filling

     Zest of 1 large lime or 2 smaller ones
½   cup freshly squeezed lime juice*
2⅓   cups powdered sugar (300 grams or 10½ ounces)
4   large eggs
3   tablespoons all-purpose flour (35 grams or 1¼ ounces)
½   teaspoon baking powder
     Powdered sugar to finish

*It will take about 3 large limes to make ½ cup juice.

Using a microplane grater, zest the lime or limes. Squeeze the juice from the limes to make ½ cup juice.

Place all the ingredients in a clean processor bowl and process just to mix completely. Do not overmix as you don't want to incorporate a lot of air.

Pour mixture over the cheesecake layer and bake for about 18 minutes until set. Cool completely.

Release the sides of the bars with a metal spatula. Refrigerate until cold, then cut bars 6 across and 4 down.

If serving immediately, dust lightly with powdered sugar and serve at room temperature. If making ahead, wait to dust until serving.

Yield: 24 bars

Storage: Store covered in the refrigerator for about 5 days without powdered sugar. These also freeze well without powdered sugar. Thaw frozen bars in the refrigerator overnight and serve at room temperature dusted with powdered sugar. ◆

Rugelach Bars

I FELL IN LOVE WITH rugelach when I was working on the cookie book. The original book contained an additional seventy recipes for European cookies, and rugelach was one of them. When the decision was made to split the book into two volumes, with the European cookie book following this American one, I designed these bars as a quick and easy version to include here.

The pastry dough for the Rugelach Bars is easy to make and just as easy to roll out, with no need for chilling if made in the food processor. Two pieces of pastry are sandwiched with a filling of jam, walnuts, cinnamon, and sugar. Any jam or any nut can be used; however, if the preserves have pieces of fruit, it should be processed or blended to smooth out before using here.

Rugelach Pastry

2¼ cups all-purpose flour (315 grams or about 11 ounces)
½ teaspoon salt
1 cup unsalted butter* (225 grams, 8 ounces, or 2 sticks)

8 ounces cream cheese* (225 grams or 1 package)
¼ cup sour cream (60 grams, about 2 ounces)

*Cold and cut into small pieces for the processor method. Softened for the mixer method.

Processor Method: Place the flour and salt in the bowl of a processor. Pulse several times to mix.

Place cold cut up butter and cream cheese over the flour. Dollop the sour cream on top. Pulse until the pastry looks crumbly but sticks together when pressed between your fingers. It should not form a ball.

Mixer Method: Whisk together the flour and salt.

Place softened butter and cream cheese, along with the sour cream, in the bowl of a mixer and beat until completely combined. Add flour mixture and beat on low speed until crumbly.

Assembly

Preheat the oven to 375°F /190°C. Spray a 9x13x2 inch pan or quarter sheet pan with a non-stick baking release and set aside.

1¼ cups walnuts or any nut (140 grams or 5 ounces)
    Rugelach Pastry, above
¾ cup red plum jam or any flavor jam*
1½ tablespoons granulated sugar
1½ teaspoons cinnamon
1 large egg white, beaten
    Sanding sugar, as needed

*Whatever jam you like can be used. If using preserves, puree them in a processor or blender to smooth.

Toast the nuts for 7 to 10 minutes, depending upon the size of the nuts. Cool completely. Chop coarsely.

Turn out the dough onto the work surface.

Push it together, and knead into a cohesive dough.

If it is too soft to easily roll, refrigerate until firm. Divide the dough in half (about 410 grams or 14⅓ ounces each).

Roll one piece into a 9½ x 13 inch rectangle. Roll the second piece into a 9 x 12½ inch rectangle. Refrigerate this second piece.

Place the larger piece of dough into the bottom of the prepared pan. Press the edges up against the sides of the pan about ¼".

Bake for 25 minutes until lightly browned and baked through. It may appear cracked, but that is fine. Cool the crust.

Spread the jam over the crust. Top with the toasted nuts.

Combine the granulated sugar and cinnamon, and sprinkle over the nuts. Place the refrigerated piece of dough over the top and press it down gently over the nuts. Make sure the dough adheres to the sides of the pan.

Whisk the egg white and brush it lightly onto the pastry. Sprinkle well with sanding sugar. Cut through the **top piece of dough only** into 6 or 7 across and 4 down, or whatever size you wish.

Bake for 35 to 40 minutes until golden brown. Cool about 10 minutes, then release the edges with a metal spatula. Turn out onto a cake board and turn right side up. Cut the bars all the way through following the cuts on top. Clean the knife between cuts. Cool completely.

Yield: 24 to 28 bars

Storage: Store at room temperature in a covered container for up to a week. These can also be be frozen well-wrapped for several months - simply unwrap and thaw on a rack at room temperature. ◆

Chapter 7
Brownies

BROWNIES ARE MUCH LOVED AND for very good reason. They can be very, very simple (so much so that my five-year-old grandson could make one of these), and also more complex for those who like to add a bit more to these most-loved cookies. I know there must be somebody out there that doesn't like brownies... but I have yet to find them!

Mocha Kahlua Brownies

Demarco's Brownies

Loaded Brownies

Frosted Brownies

Santa Fe Brownies

Amaretto Brownies

Macadamia White Chocolate Lightening-Fast Brownies

Turtle Brownies

My Cocoa Brownies

Mocha Kahlua Brownies

THESE BROWNIES WERE ONE OF our bestsellers at the bakery. They are amazingly easy, and I could eat the frosting by the spoonful (and often did). We trimmed the edges before we cut them, and my staff and I would devour them.

Mocha Kahlua Brownies

6	tablespoons unsalted butter (90 grams, 3 ounces, or ¾ stick)
9	ounces semisweet chocolate (255 grams)
5	large eggs
2¼	cups granulated sugar (450 grams or 1 pound)
1½	tablespoons warm water
1½	tablespoons instant coffee
1¼	cup all-purpose flour (175 grams or 6 ounces)

Preheat the oven to 350°F / 175°C. Line the bottom of a 9x13x2 inch pan or a quarter sheet pan with parchment paper. Spray with a non-stick baking release. Set aside.

Melt the butter and chocolate over a double broiler or in the microwave at half power. Whisk to combine and smooth.

Place the eggs and sugar in the bowl of a mixer, and mix on low speed until well combined.

In a small bowl, dissolve the coffee in the water. Add to the sugar mixture, mixing on low speed until completely incorporated. Scrape the sides and bottom of the bowl well and add the melted chocolate. Mix well on low. Finally, add the flour on low speed. Scrape the sides and bottom of the bowl, and mix again.

Pour the batter into the prepared pan and smooth the top. Bake for 30 to 35 minutes until a cake tester comes out with moist crumbs. Cool completely.

Mocha Kahlua Frosting

3	ounces semisweet chocolate (85 grams)
½	cup unsalted butter, softened (114 grams, 4 ounces, or 1 stick)
1¼	cups sifted powdered sugar (160 grams or 5⅔ ounces)
1	tablespoon Kahlua liqueur
¼	cup clear corn syrup

Melt the chocolate and set aside to cool to room temperature.

Combine the remaining ingredients in a mixing bowl. Beat to mix well. Add the melted chocolate and beat until very light in color and the volume has increased.

Release the brownie base from the pan by turning it upside down onto a cake board. Remove the parchment paper. Keeping them bottom side up, spread the frosting on the brownies and refrigerate until firm. Cut 3 across 5 down with a hot dry knife.

Yield: 15 brownies

Storage: Keep for days in a covered container at room temperature. These may also be frozen well-wrapped for months. Thaw on a rack at room temperature. ◆

Demarco's Brownies

AT THE BAKERY, WHEN WORK was slow in the summer, I would encourage my employees to create desserts of their own. Demarco Howard worked with me for years, and while I was sad to see him leave, I knew the time had come for him to move on. This brownie was one he created, and it is as special as he is.

The base of this brownie is as fudgy and chocolatey as it gets. Then, a cream cheese and raspberry filling is topped with an old-fashioned oatmeal streusel.

Demarco's creation takes brownies to another level. Because they are so rich, I cut these smaller than most brownies.

These brownies bake in a 10x14x2 inch pan, often referred to as a lasagna pan. They take up every inch!

Crumb Topping

¾ cup old-fashioned oats (58 grams or 2 ounces)

½ cup packed light or dark brown sugar (100 grams or 3½ ounces)

½ cup walnuts, chopped (60 grams or 2 ounces)

¼ teaspoon cinnamon

⅛ teaspoon salt

½ cup all-purpose flour (70 grams or about 2½ ounces)

6 tablespoons unsalted butter, cold and cut into small pieces (90 grams, 3 ounces, or ¾ stick)

Place all ingredients in the bowl of a mixer. Mix to combine until there are large moist crumbs. Do not overmix or it will completely combine. Refrigerate while preparing the rest of the recipe.

Brownie Base

¾ cup unsalted butter (170 grams, 6 ounces, or 1½ sticks)

8 ounces semisweet chocolate (225 grams)

4 large eggs

1½ teaspoons vanilla extract

1 cup packed light or dark brown sugar (200 grams or 7 ounces)

¾ cup granulated sugar (150 grams or 5⅓ ounces)

1 cup all-purpose flour (140 grams or 5 ounces)

1 teaspoon baking powder

½ teaspoon salt

Preheat the oven to 350°F / 175°C. Spray the bottom of a 10x14x2 inch pan with non-stick baking release and line with parchment paper. Spray the entire pan and set it aside.

Melt the butter and chocolate over a double broiler or in the microwave at half power. Whisk to combine and smooth. Cool to lukewarm.

Beat the eggs, vanilla, and both sugars together until combined. Mix in the melted chocolate.

Whisk together the flour, baking powder, and salt. Add to the chocolate mixture, beating on low speed just until everything is blended.

Spread the batter evenly in the prepared pan, and chill to firm.

Brownie Filling and Assembly
Brownie base
½   cup seedless red raspberry jam
12   ounces cream cheese (340 grams)
¾   cup granulated sugar (150 grams or 5⅓ ounces)
1½   teaspoons vanilla extract
3   large eggs
Crumb topping

Spread the raspberry jam over the brownie base.

Place the cream cheese, sugar, vanilla, and eggs in the bowl of a processor. Process until completely smooth, scraping the bowl several times. Pour mixture over the jam.

Distribute the crumb topping evenly over the top of the filling. Press in lightly.

Bake for 55 to 65 minutes until it is a little wiggly in the middle. Cool completely in the pan. Release

the edges using a flexible metal spatula and refrigerate until cold.

Go around the edges of the pan again to loosen. Place a cake board on top and turn the brownies over. If they do not come out, warm the sides and bottom of the pan with a blow dryer set on high (see page xxxix for technique). Remove the parchment paper and turn right side up.

Cut 6 across and 5 down.

Yield: 30 brownies

Storage: These keep well at room temperature the first day. After that, cover and refrigerate for 5 days or freeze well-wrapped for longer storage. Thaw in the refrigerator and serve at room temperature. ◆

Loaded Brownies

A FUDGY BROWNIE TOPPED WITH caramel, two kinds of chocolate chips, and peanuts - that's as good as any brownie can get. These were the second bestselling brownie at the bakery.

Caramel
1   Recipe Best Caramel Ever, cooked to 240°F / 116°C, see page xxix

Loaded Brownies
½   cup unsalted butter (114 grams, 4 ounces, or 1 stick)
6   ounces semisweet chocolate (170 grams)
3   large eggs
1½   cups granulated sugar (300 grams or 10½ ounces)
1   teaspoon vanilla extract
¾   cup all-purpose flour (105 grams or 3½ ounce)
4   ounces chopped peanuts (114 grams)
¾   cup milk chocolate chips (140 grams or 5 ounces)
¾   cup semisweet chocolate chips (140 grams or 5 ounces)
Caramel (above)

Preheat the oven to 350°F /175°C. Line a 9x13x2 inch pan or a quarter sheet pan with foil and spray with a non-stick baking release, then line with parchment paper and spray again. This double lining is necessary as the caramel will stick like crazy. Set aside.

Melt the butter and chocolate over a double broiler or in the microwave at half power. Whisk to combine and smooth. Set aside.

Combine the eggs and sugar in the bowl of a mixer and beat to mix well. Add the melted chocolate and beat well. Add the vanilla and flour, beating just to mix.

Remove the bowl from the mixer and stir from the bottom up to make sure everything is incorporated. Stir in the peanuts and both chocolate chips. Spread the batter evenly into the prepared pan.

Briefly microwave the caramel until spreadable. Dollop over the brownie batter and swirl in with a metal spatula.

If using a quarter sheet pan, place it on a half sheet pan to make it easier to move in and out of the oven. Bake for 25 to 30 minutes. The brownies will be very wiggly, that is as it should be. Cool completely, then chill to firm the caramel.

To release the brownies, turn the brownies out onto a cake board. Remove the foil and parchment paper. Turn right side up.

Cut 4 across and 5 or 6 down, rinsing the knife under hot water and drying with each cut. Serve at room temperature.

Yield: 20 to 24 brownies

Storage: Keep in a closed container for 5 to 7 days at room temperature or freeze well-wrapped for longer storage. Thaw and serve at room temperature. ◆

Frosted Brownies

I LOVE BROWNIES, ESPECIALLY THE fudgy ones, but this particular brownie is neither fudgy nor cakey. It is somewhere in between, making them the ideal brownie to frost. These are easy enough to whip up on the spur of the moment. They can also be enhanced with nuts or chocolate chips if desired.

Brownies

7   ounces semisweet chocolate, chopped (200 grams)

¾   cup butter, cut into small pieces (170 grams or 6 ounces)

1½   cups granulated sugar (300 grams or 10½ ounces)

3   tablespoons cocoa, natural or Dutch (20 grams or about ⅔ ounce)

2   teaspoons vanilla extract

4   large eggs

1   cup all-purpose flour (140 grams or 5 ounces)

¾   cup chocolate chips or nuts, optional (130 grams or 4½ ounces)

Preheat the oven to 350°F / 175°C. Spray a 9x9x2 inch pan with a non-stick baking release and line with parchment paper. Spray the pan and the parchment paper and set aside.

Melt the chocolate and butter over a double broiler or in the microwave at half power. In the meantime, sift the sugar and cocoa together. Set aside.

Place the melted chocolate mixture into the bowl of a mixer. Add the sugar/cocoa mixture and mix on low speed until combined. Add the vanilla and eggs, beating on low speed to blend. Add the flour, again mixing on low. Add the chocolate chips or nuts if using.

Pour batter into the prepared pan and smooth the top. Bake for about 30 minutes until a tester comes out with moist crumbs.

Cool completely before frosting.

Chocolate Frosting

⅓   cup unsalted butter (75 grams, 2⅔ ounces, or 5 tablespoons)

2   ounces semisweet chocolate (60 grams)

2   cups powdered sugar (260 grams or 9⅛ ounces)

2　teaspoons vanilla extract
1　to 2 tablespoons milk

Melt the butter and chocolate together over a double boiler or in the microwave at half power. Whisk to combine and smooth. Cool to lukewarm.

Place the melted chocolate in a mixing bowl with the powdered sugar, vanilla, and 1 tablespoon of milk. Beat on low speed just to bring together.

Raise the speed of the mixer, and beat to lighten and increase the volume. If necessary, add additional milk to make a spreadable consistency. Spread the frosting over the top of the brownies. Allow to set. Cut 4 across and 4 down.

Yield: 16 brownies

Storage: Store in a covered container at room temperature for about 5 days. These also freeze extremely well for several months - Freeze after frosting, whole or cut, and wrap well. Thaw on a rack and serve at room temperature. ◆

Santa Fe Brownies

WE COULDN'T MAKE ENOUGH OF these brownies at the bakery. When we brought on a large chain of grocery stores, Demarco (my baker) had to make twelve pans, twice a day, to get everyone started. I remember it so well… Once early on, at the end of a long day, he came up to me and half-heartedly said, "You sure know how to make a person want to quit." I was happy to see him the next morning and many afterward, ready and willing to take on any task.

We made them exactly as instructed in the recipe below. While these are not the quickest brownies to make, they certainly are the best.

The original recipe came from Maida Heatter's "Best Dessert Book Ever," with a few changes. I have no idea how they got their Santa Fe name, but you could call them anything and they would still be the best.

Brownie Layer

1½ cups all-purpose flour (210 grams or 7⅓ ounces)
1½ teaspoon baking powder
¾ teaspoon salt
1 cup unsalted butter (225 grams, 8 ounces, or 2 sticks)
12 ounces semisweet chocolate (340 grams)
5 large eggs
1½ cups packed light or dark brown sugar (300 grams or 10½ ounces)
1 cup + 2 tablespoons granulated sugar (225 grams or 8 ounces)
1 tablespoon vanilla extract
1 cup walnuts, coarsely chopped (114 grams or 4 ounces)

Preheat the oven to 350°F / 175°C. Line the bottom of a 9x13x2 inch pan with parchment paper. Spray the paper and sides of pan with a non-stick baking release. Set aside.

Whisk together the flour, baking powder, and salt. Set aside.

Melt the butter and chocolate over a double broiler or in the microwave at half power. Whisk to combine and smooth.

Place the eggs, both sugars, and vanilla in a mixing bowl and mix on low speed. Add the melted chocolate and mix well. Add the flour mixture and mix on low. Scrape the sides of the bowl often to make sure the flour is completely incorporated.

Divide the batter evenly between 2 bowls (about 775 grams or 27⅛ ounces per bowl). Stir the wal-

nuts into one bowl, and spread this chocolate-walnut batter evenly in the bottom of the prepared pan.

Place the second bowl of brownie batter (without the nuts) over a double boiler over simmering, not boiling, water. Stir frequently. This keeps this portion of batter fluid enough to swirl in. Make the cheesecake layer while this heats.

Cheesecake Layer

12 ounces cream cheese, softened (340 grams)
6 tablespoons unsalted butter, softened (90 grams, 3 ounces, or ¾ stick)
¾ cup granulated sugar (150 grams or 5⅓ ounces)
1½ teaspoon vanilla extract
3 large eggs

In the bowl of a processor or mixer, combine the cream cheese, butter, and sugar. Process until smooth. Add the vanilla and eggs, processing until thoroughly mixed. Scrape down the sides of the bowl and process to eliminate any lumps.

Assembly

Chocolate-walnut brownie layer in the pan
Cheesecake layer
Bowl of warm brownie layer

Spread the cheesecake layer over the chocolate-walnut base layer.

The heated brownie mixture should be hot enough to be poured but not runny. It should be thick enough to sit on top of the cheesecake layer and not sink to the bottom. If you have doubts, test in a small section. If it sinks, let the batter cool a bit to thicken. When ready, pour over the cheesecake layer around the edges, leaving the middle without chocolate.

With a spatula, lift the cheesecake layer up and over the chocolate to create a marbleized pattern. Swirl the spatula through several times.

Lift the pan about 3 or 4 inches off the table and drop the pan one time. Bake for 50 to 60 minutes, turning the pan halfway through if necessary. The top will be lightly browned - do not overbake. Cool completely.

Go around the edges of the pan with a spatula to loosen. Turn the brownies out of the pan onto a cake board. Remove the parchment paper, turn right side up, and refrigerate until cold. Cut four across and five down.

Yield: 20 brownies

Storage: Keep in the refrigerator in an airtight container for 6 or 7 days. Alternatively, these can be frozen well-wrapped for several months. Thaw on a rack and serve at room temperature. ◆

Amaretto Brownies

USE YOUR IMAGINATION, AND ANY liqueur, to flavor this versatile brownie in endless ways. And if that isn't enough to entice you, these are also so easy, coming together in minutes. A portion of the chocolate base is reserved to make the crumb topping, sandwiching a cream cheese layer in the middle.

Chocolate Base

1⅔ cups all-purpose flour (230 grams or about 8 ounces)
1 cup granulated sugar (200 grams or 7 ounces)
⅔ cup Dutch cocoa (60 grams or 2 ounces)
½ cup unsalted butter, cold and cut into small pieces (114 grams, 4 ounces, or 1 stick)
1 large egg

Preheat the oven to 350°F / 175°C. Line the bottom of a quarter sheet pan or a 9x13 inch pan with parchment paper. Spray the paper and sides of the pan with a non-stick baking release. Set aside.

Place the flour, sugar, and cocoa in the bowl of a processor. Process to mix well. Add the cold butter, and process until the butter is indistinguishable. **Remove 1¼ cups** (160 grams or 4½ ounces). Set aside.

Add the egg to the processor bowl and process until large crumbs form, redistributing once or twice. Spread the crumbs evenly in the bottom of the prepared pan and press in firmly. Set aside.

Filling

8 ounces cream cheese, softened (225 grams)
1 14-ounce can of condensed milk
1 large egg
¼ cup amaretto or liqueur of choice
1 teaspoon almond extract
1 tablespoon unsalted butter, melted
  Reserved crumb mixture from above
½ cup sliced almonds (45 grams or 1½ ounces)

Wipe the processor bowl clean with a paper towel. Cut the cream cheese into 3 or 4 pieces, and place them in the bowl of the processor. Process until smooth, scraping down once or twice.

Add the condensed milk, egg, amaretto, and almond extract. Process to mix well, scraping down the sides of the bowl to make sure there are no lumps. Pour filling over the chocolate base.

Add the melted butter to the reserved crumb mixture. Mix with a fork until the crumbs are coated. I usually resort to mixing by hand towards the end. Add the sliced almonds and mix to combine. Distribute evenly over the cream cheese filling.

Bake for 25 to 30 minutes until set. Cool for about 10 minutes, then go around the edges with a metal spatula to loosen the sides. Leave in the pan and refrigerate until cold, preferably overnight.

When ready to cut, loosen the sides again with a metal spatula. Turn out onto a cake board, flip right side up, and cut 4 across and 5 down.

Yield: 20 brownies

Storage: Serve at room temperature, but store well-covered in the refrigerator where they will last for about a week. Freeze well-wrapped for longer storage. Thaw in the refrigerator. ◆

Macadamia White Chocolate Lightening-Fast Brownies

Honestly, these brownies come under the category of "embarrassingly easy to make." A few measuring utensils, a bowl, and a whisk are all that is needed. In fact, they are so easy that my five-year-old grandson made them. He just kept whisking and whisking, and as we neared the end, he looked up and said, "These are really hard, Grandma." But

whisk away he did, and was very proud of the baked brownies.

Macadamia White Chocolate Lightening-Fast Brownies

½   cup unsalted butter (114 grams, 4 ounces, or 1 stick)
4   ounces semisweet chocolate (114 grams)
1   cup granulated sugar (200 grams or 7 ounces)
1   teaspoon vanilla extract
¼   teaspoon salt
2   large eggs
½   cup all-purpose flour (70 grams or about 2½ ounces)

Preheat the oven to 375°F / 190°C. Line an 8x8x2 inch pan with parchment paper. Spray the paper and pan with a non-stick baking release. Set aside.

Melt together the butter and chocolate over a double boiler or in the microwave at half power. Whisk to combine and smooth.

Whisk in the sugar, vanilla, and salt. Add the eggs and whisk again. Add the flour and stir to mix completely.

Pour into the prepared pan. Bake for 25 to 30 minutes until set and moist crumbs cling to a tester.

Ganache Glaze
½   cup 40% cream
4   ounces semisweet chocolate (114 grams)
⅓   cup macadamia nuts, coarsely chopped (about 40 grams or 1½ ounces)
⅓   cup white chocolate, coarsely chopped (about 55 ounces or 2 ounces)

In a saucepan, heat the cream until steaming, but

do not boil. Remove from the heat. Submerge the semisweet chocolate under the cream. Let sit for several minutes, then whisk gently until combined and smooth.

Pour the glaze over the baked brownies, and spread to the edges. Immediately sprinkle the nuts and white chocolate over the top. Refrigerate to set the glaze.

Release the brownies from the pan. Cut 4 across and 4 down.

Yield: 16 brownies

Storage: After the chocolate glaze has set, store covered at room temperature for 3 to 4 days. Freeze for longer storage.

Make Ahead: The brownies can be made ahead and frozen. Thaw at room temperature, then add the glaze, macadamia nuts, and white chocolate.

Variations:

Basic Lightening-Fast Brownies: Omit the nuts and white chocolate topping.

Snickers Lightening-Fast Brownies: Omit the nuts and white chocolate topping. Coarsely chop nearly-frozen Snickers bars and sprinkle over the top of the glaze. Any candy bar can be used. ◆

Turtle Brownies

THESE TURTLE BROWNIES FEATURE A cake-like chocolate base with a cream cheese ripple. Caramel, chocolate ganache, and toasted pecans take this treat to the top of the "must try" list.

The caramel can be made up to a week in advance making this easier to put together.

Caramel
1   recipe Best Caramel Ever, page xxix

Cream Cheese Ripple
9   ounces cream cheese (255 grams)
3   tablespoons unsalted butter, softened (45 grams or 1½ ounces)
¼   cup + 2 tablespoons granulated sugar (75 grams or 2⅔ ounces)
1   large egg
1   large egg yolk

Place the cream cheese, butter, and sugar in the bowl of a processor. Process until smooth, scraping the sides of the bowl several times. Add the egg and yolk, and process until completely blended. Set aside.

Chocolate Base

1   cup + 3 tablespoons Dutch cocoa (105 grams or 3¾ ounces)

1⅓   cups all-purpose flour (185 grams or 6½ ounces)

½   teaspoon baking powder

½   teaspoon salt

6   tablespoons unsalted butter, softened (90 grams, 3 ounces, or ¾ stick)

1⅞   cups granulated sugar (375 grams or 13½ ounces)

3   large eggs

½   cup water

Preheat the oven to 350°F / 175°C. Line the bottom of a 9x13x2 inch pan with parchment paper. Spray the paper and pan with a non-stick baking release. Set aside.

Sift the cocoa, flour, baking powder, and salt together. Set aside.

Place the butter and sugar in the bowl of a mixer. Beat to combine, scraping the sides as necessary. Add the eggs and water, and beat to combine. Add the flour mixture and beat on low speed until completely incorporated.

Spread evenly in the prepared pan. Dollop the cream cheese mixture over the chocolate batter and lightly swirl it through.

Bake for 30 to 35 minutes until a tester comes out clean. Do not overbake. Cool and release the base from the pan.

Caramel Layer

    Baked chocolate base

    Best Caramel Ever

Briefly microwave the caramel to soften. Spread over the top of the base. Chill to set up.

Cream Glaze Finish

¾   cup heavy cream

6   ounces semisweet chocolate (170 grams)

½   cup toasted pecan pieces

In a saucepan, heat the cream until very hot but not boiling. Submerge the chocolate under the cream and let it sit for a few minutes. Whisk very gently until smooth.

Spread chocolate glaze over the caramel layer and sprinkle with toasted pecans. Refrigerate.

Using a knife dipped in hot water and quickly dried, trim the brownie edges and cut 5 across and 4 down.

Yield: 20 brownies

Storage: Store in the refrigerator in an airtight container for up to 5 days. Freeze for longer storage - Thaw in the refrigerator and serve at room temperature. ◆

My Cocoa Brownies

COCOA BROWNIES HAVE NEVER BEEN in my wheelhouse and I'm not sure why; but I have a sneaking suspicion that I am simply prejudiced in favor of chocolate. However, while wandering around online, an article on cocoa brownies caught my eye.

The original recipe comes from the "Kitchn" blog, and are called "Pantry Cocoa Brownies." They have a very particular method of putting the brownies together. I added the ingredients in the order stated, I mixed as long as the recipe indicated, and into the oven the Cocoa Brownies went.

While I was waiting for them to bake, I wondered what would happen if I just mixed them in the traditional way, without all of the stated times and specified order. This is exactly what usually gets me into trouble.

You guessed it - I scaled all of the ingredients and put them together in a much faster way of mixing. But what happened surprised me… The original brownies came out about ½" thick with a very shiny paper-thin top. My version came out about ¾" thick, with the same shiny thin top, but with a lighter and less dense texture. Not by a ton, but definitely noticeable.

I used exactly the same ingredients, but simply put them together differently. Either way, they are a winner. I'm so happy I found them, and I think you will be too!

My Cocoa Brownies

⅔   cup natural cocoa (55 grams or 2 scant ounces)
½   cup all-purpose flour (70 grams or about 2½ ounces)
½   teaspoon salt
¼   teaspoon baking powder
3   large eggs
⅔   cup packed dark brown sugar (130 grams or 4½ ounces)
1⅓ cup powdered sugar (170 grams or 6 ounces)
⅔   cup canola or vegetable oil
1   teaspoon vanilla extract

Preheat the oven to 325°F /163°C. Line the bottom of a 9" square pan with parchment paper. Spray the paper and sides of the pan with a non-stick baking release. Set aside.

Sift the cocoa, flour, salt, and baking powder through a strainer. The cocoa has a tendency to lump together and not want to dissolve in liquid. Sifting takes care of that problem.

Place the eggs and both sugars in the bowl of a mixer, and beat for about 3 minutes or until fluffy and lighter in color. Add the oil and vanilla, mixing until completely combined. Add the flour mixture and beat on low speed just to combine.

Pour the batter into the prepared pan and smooth the top. Bake for 28 to 33 minutes until a tester comes out with moist crumbs. Cool.

Loosen the edges with a spatula and turn out the brownies. Cut 4 across and 4 down.

That's it, Cocoa Brownies in no time!

Yield: 16 brownies

Storage: These will last several days in a closed container at room temperature.

Make Ahead: Because these are so easy, I usually make them as needed. However, they will freeze well, simply thaw on a rack at room temperature.

Variation: For **Mexican Cocoa Brownies**, add 2 teaspoons cinnamon to the cocoa/flour mixture. ◆

Craving Cookies Index

About the Author

BEFORE SETTING OUT ON HER career in food, Helen S. Fletcher was happily making a home for her husband, T. Mike Fletcher and their two sons. Food and entertaining were an important part of that life and it soon became evident that baking and pastry would be the dominant interest for the rest of her life.

While writing for newspapers and magazines, she was invited to spend time in the Cuisinart's test kitchen after which she became a consultant to them in their formative days.

Her first book, *The New Pastry Cook,* followed after which she opened her wholesale bakery, Truffes, servicing hotels, restaurants and caterers. With no experience in either professional baking or business the bakery grew at a rapid pace expanding twice in four years. Known for quality, consistency and service, her clients appreciated her dedication to using the best ingredients and baking in small batches to ensure the quality.

After 25 years, Helen closed the bakery and found retirement didn't suit her so she became the pastry chef at St. Louis' most esteemed restaurant, Tony's, where she continues in that capacity today.

Her blog, Pastries Like a Pro (www.pastrieslikeapro.com) shares the techniques and knowledge she has gained in her 30 years of professional baking. ◆